Oracle Certification Prep

Study Guide for

1Z0-063: Oracle Database 12c: Advanced Administration

Matthew Morris

Study Guide for Oracle Database 12c: Advanced Administration (Exam 1Z0-063) Rev 1.0

ISBN-13: 978-1-941404-04-1
ISBN-10: 1941404049

Table of Contents

What to Expect from the Test

The test consists of 80 multiple choice or multiple answer questions and you have 120 minutes to complete it. The passing score listed on Oracle Education at this time is 60%, but as with all Oracle certification tests, they note it is subject to change. For multiple-answer questions, you must provide all of the correct answers to get credit for the question. Answer every question on the exam – an unanswered question counts off the same amount as an incorrect one. Take your time reading the question and all of the answers. Sometimes later questions will answer earlier ones and I have found that marking questions I'm not sure of and re-reading them again at the end of the test is valuable.

The Administration II exam underwent massive changes between 11g and 12c. Essentially everything that was not related to preventing loss of data has been moved out of this exam in order to make room for new sections on the Multitenant architecture. The 1Z0-063 exam is about 60% data protection (mostly backup & recovery) and 40% Multitenant. If you do not know RMAN and the new CDB-based architecture, you will not pass this test.

To prepare for this exam, you need to install a 12c database and try out the Multitentant architecture. Create some pluggable databases and play around with common users and roles. Backup of PDBs, unplug them and plug them back in. All of these tasks did not exist until 12c, so if you have never worked with the database, you cannot understand how they work yet.

Even more important than understanding Multitenant, however, is comprehensive knowledge of RMAN. Preventing the loss of data is one of the cardinal responsibilities of a senior database administrator. Recovery Manager is the most important tool in meeting that responsibility and this test is designed to make sure you understand how to use it effectively. Knowledge of RMAN will help you on the test and it will be critical if you are ever in charge of administrating an Oracle database.

What to Expect from this Study Guide

This guide is built around the subject matter topics that Oracle Education has indicated will be tested. The guide covers a significant percentage of the information and operations that you must be familiar with in order to pass the exam. It is designed to present the information in a condensed format, so the information is often presented without much context. The guide presents information that you are likely to need for the exam, but seldom gets into the detail of why a DBA needs to know this information.

It is critical for you to work with the database as part of your study process. No book in and of itself is a substitute for hands-on experience. In preparing for this exam, you should install and configure an Oracle 12c database, create users and tables, and use RMAN to create backups and perform restore operations. Practicing the concepts discussed on this guide on your own database prior to scheduling your exam will increase the probability of success greatly.

The goal of this guide is to present to you the concepts and information most likely to be the subject of test questions, and to do so in a very compact format that will allow you to read through it more than once to reinforce the information. If much of the information presented in this guide is completely new to you, then you need to supplement this guide with other sources of study materials. If you have a reasonable grounding in Oracle administration tasks, then the guide will serve to reinforce those portions that you will likely be questioned about on the exam. If you don't have any experience with Oracle at all, the compressed format of this guide is not likely to be the best method for learning. It might provide you with sufficient information to pass the test, but you're likely to have serious deficiencies as an Oracle database administrator. If much of the information presented is completely new to you -- then you need to supplement this guide with other source of study materials to build a firm foundation of Oracle knowledge. I highly recommend using the materials at the companion website of this series that is discussed in the next section.

Additional Study Resources

The companion website to this series is www.oraclecertificationprep.com. The site contains many additional resources that can be used to study for this exam (and others). From the entry page of the website, click on the 'Exams' button, and then select the link for this test. The Exam Details page contains links to the following information sources:

- Applicable Oracle documentation.
- Third-party books relevant to the exam.
- White papers and articles on Oracle Learning Library on topics covered in the exam.
- Articles on the Web that may be useful for the exam.
- Videos at YouTube and other sites that provide relevant tutorials.

The website will never link to unauthorized content such as brain dumps or illegal content such as copyrighted material made available without the consent of the author. I cannot guarantee the accuracy of the content links. While I have located the data and scanned it to ensure that it is relevant to the given exam, I did not write it and have not proofread it from a technical standpoint. The material on the Oracle Learning Library is almost certain to be completely accurate and most of the other links come from highly popular Oracle support websites and are created by experienced Oracle professionals.

I recommend that you use more than one source of study materials whenever you are preparing for a certification. Reading information presented from multiple different viewpoints can help to give you a more complete picture of any given topic. The links on the website can help you to do this. Fully understanding the information covered in this certification is not just valuable so that getting a passing score is more likely – it will also help you in your career. I guarantee that in the long run, any knowledge you gain while studying for this certification will provide more benefit to you than any piece of paper or line on your resume.

Oracle Database 12c: Backup and Recovery

Oracle Data Protection Solutions

Explain Oracle backup and recovery solutions

One of the primary duties of an Oracle database administrator is to design, implement, and manage a backup and recovery strategy. A well-designed backup strategy should protect the database against data loss and provide the ability to reconstruct the database in the event of a failure that involves damage or destruction to the data. The tasks of backup administrators can include the following:

- Planning and testing responses to different kinds of failures
- Configuring the database environment for backup and recovery
- Setting up a backup schedule
- Monitoring the backup and recovery environment
- Troubleshooting backup problems
- Recovering from data loss if the need arises
- Data archival, which involves creating a database copy for long-term storage
- Data transfer, which involves moving data from one database or one host to another

There are a number of third-party backup solutions available that can be used to back up an Oracle database. However, they are outside the scope of the topic. The three backup and recovery options that can be used with native Oracle capabilities include:

- **Recovery Manager (RMAN)** -- Oracle's Recovery Manager is fully integrated with the Oracle Database. It can perform a wide range of tasks and can automate much of the backup and recovery process. RMAN can be accessed through the command line or through Oracle Enterprise Manager.

- **Enterprise Manager Cloud Control** -- EM Cloud Control provides a web-based front end and scheduling facilities for RMAN. From the web interface, it is possible to enter job parameters and specify a job schedule. From this, Cloud Control will execute RMAN to conduct the backup and recovery operations.
- **User-managed backup and recovery** -- With user-managed backup and recovery, the database administrator will use a mixture of host operating system commands and SQL*Plus recovery commands to back up and recovery the files that make up an Oracle database. The DBA is responsible for determining all aspects of when and how backups and recovery are done.

User-managed recovery is supported by Oracle and is fully documented. However, RMAN is the preferred solution. It provides a common interface for backup tasks across different host operating systems. There are a number of backup techniques that are available through RMAN that cannot be performed when utilizing user-managed methods.

Describe types of database failures

There are a number of different problems that can affect the normal operation of an Oracle database or impair database I/O operations. However, the failures that require DBA intervention and data repair generally fall into one of three categories: user errors, application errors, and media failures.

- **User Errors** – These occur when data in your database is changed or deleted incorrectly through the actions of users. The root cause might be an error in application logic or a manual mistake. An example would be when a user drops a database table by mistake.
- **Application Errors** – It is possible for a software malfunction to corrupt data blocks. If this takes the form of a physical corruption (also known as a media corruption), the database does not recognize the block.

- **Media Failures** – In a media failure, a problem external to the database prevents it from reading from or writing to a database file while the instance is running. Common media failures include disk failures and the deletion of database files.

There are other failure classes. However, these do not typically result in the need for DBA intervention or media recovery:

- **Statement Failure** – If a SQL statement fails, all changes made by it will be automatically rolled back. The failure of a single SQL statement will not impact other statements in the transaction.
- **User Process Failure** – If a user session or process fails, PMON will automatically detect this and clean up after it. Any transactions that were active at the time of the failure will be rolled back and all locks held will be released.
- **Instance Failure** – If the database instance fails or is shut down with the ABORT clause, the database will perform instance recovery on the next startup.

Describe the tools available for backup and recovery tasks

The tool provided by Oracle to handle backup and recovery tasks is Recovery Manager (RMAN). RMAN is an Oracle Database client application that provides a command-line interface. It automates the administration of the backup strategy for an Oracle database and can be used to perform backup and recovery tasks. The elements of the RMAN environment include:

- **Target database** -- This is an Oracle Database to which RMAN is connected with the TARGET keyword. This is the database for which RMAN is performing backup and recovery operations.

- **RMAN client** -- The RMAN executable is installed along with an Oracle database, generally in the same directory as the other database executables. This database interprets commands from RMAN and directs server sessions to execute those commands.
- **Fast recovery area** -- Optionally, this disk location can be used to store and manage files related to backup and recovery.
- **Media management** -- Software is required if RMAN must interact with sequential media devices such as tape libraries.
- **Recovery catalog** -- When used, this is a database schema used to record RMAN activity against one or more target databases. It will preserve RMAN repository metadata if the control file of the target database is lost

If RMAN is not used for backup and recovery, it is possible to make use of third-party tools to perform this task. There are a number of such applications on the market. Generally when using third-party tools to make backups, it is necessary to use SQL or SQL*Plus commands to perform database recovery.

Describe RMAN and maximum availability architecture

Maximum Availability Architecture (MAA) is essentially the process of reducing or avoiding unplanned downtime, enabling rapid recovery from failures, and minimizing planned downtimes. RMAN plays a huge role in the second portion of that goal. When there is a database failure due to a media failure, minutes count in getting the database back online. There are several new features in RMAN with 12c designed to reduce the impact that backup and recovery operations have on availability:

- **Fine grained recovery** -- It is now possible to use a RECOVER TABLE command to perform a point-in-time recovery of a table or partition. Previously, recovering a table often required a manual point-in-time recovery process. The RECOVER TABLE command automatically performs several steps to generate an export of the table to be recovered and import it back into the production database.

- **Multitenant** -- When using the Oracle Multitenant capability, it is possible to use RMAN to perform backup and recovery at the CDB level, which includes and protects all the associated PDBs. Alternately, it is possible to perform backup and recovery for an individual PDB or a selected group of PDBs.

- **Improved RMAN duplication performance** -- Prior to 12c, the ACTIVE DUPLICATE command used production database processes to send image copies across the network. When performing ACTIVE DUPLICATE in 12c, backup sets are used instead of image copies. Because backup sets are smaller than the equivalent image copies, the information being transferred across the network is reduced. Compression and multi-section options can also be used for even faster duplication.

- **Faster Data Guard recovery** -- If there is either primary or standby datafile corruption, the recovery process prior to 12c would have been to copy the backup over the network and perform a restore/recovery. With 12c, the new RMAN keyword "FROM SERVICE" restores directly from the standby or primary depending on which site has been corrupted. The "FROM SERVICE" command creates a backup set and streams it over the network, dramatically reducing the overall recovery time.

Use the SYSBACKUP privilege

The SYSBACKUP administrative privilege has been added in Oracle 12c. This privilege is intended to allow system administrators to enable a user to perform backup and recovery of the Oracle database without providing the complete set of privileges provided by SYSDBA. SYSBACKUP provides all of the permissions required for backup and recovery including the ability to connect to a closed database. Unlike SYSDBA, someone with the SYSBACKUP privilege does not receive DBA-level data access privileges such as SELECT ANY TABLE.

In order for users to connect to a target or auxiliary database via RMAN, they must have either the SYSDBA or SYSBACKUP system privilege. Users who have been assigned to the OSBACKUPDBA operating system group can connect with the SYSBACKUP privilege via OS authentication. The following example demonstrates explicit OS Authentication using the SYSBACKUP Privilege:

```
% rman target '"/ as sysbackup"'
```

For databases that use a password file, the database creates an entry in the password file when you grant the SYSBACKUP privilege to a user. It is then possible for that user to connect to the target or auxiliary database even if the database is not open. The password file must be in the 12c format in order to support the SYSBACKUP privilege. The following example demonstrates explicit password file authentication as SYSBACKUP. The backup_admin user has been granted the SYSBACKUP privilege in the target database:

```
% rman target '"backup_admin@ocp1 as sysbackup"'
target database Password: [password]
connected to target database: OCP1 (DBID=25947551)
```

Use RMAN stand-alone and job commands

Job Commands

Job commands can only be used within the brackets of a RUN command. Some examples of job commands are:

- **ALLOCATE CHANNEL** -- Manually allocates a connection between RMAN and a database instance.

- **SWITCH** -- This is equivalent to the SQL statement ALTER DATABASE RENAME FILE. The names of the files in the RMAN repository are updated, but the database does not rename the files at the operating system level.

The RUN command is used to group a series RMAN commands into a block to be executed sequentially. RMAN will compile the list of job commands into one or more job steps and then execute the steps.

```
RUN
{
ALLOCATE CHANNEL c1 DEVICE TYPE DISK FORMAT "/u02/%U";
BACKUP DATABASE PLUS ARCHIVELOG;
}
```

Standalone Commands

Standalone commands cannot appear as subcommands within a RUN block. These commands are used directly from the RMAN prompt. Some examples include:

- **CONNECT** -- Establishes a connection between RMAN and a target, auxiliary, or recovery catalog database.
- **CONFIGURE** -- Used to create or change a persistent configuration affecting RMAN backup, restore, duplication, and maintenance jobs on a particular database.
- **CREATE CATALOG** -- Creates a recovery catalog.
- **CREATE SCRIPT** -- Creates a stored script in the recovery catalog.
- **LIST** -- Displays backups and information about other objects recorded in the RMAN repository.
- **REPORT** -- Performs detailed analyses of the RMAN repository and writes the report to standard output or the message log file.

Exceptions

A number of commands can be issued either at the prompt or within a RUN block. The following examples can function as both standalone and job commands:

- **BACKUP** -- Used to back up a primary or standby database, tablespace, data file (current or copy), control file (current or copy), server parameter file, archived redo log file, or backup set.
- **RESTORE** -- Used to restore, validate, or preview RMAN backups.
- **RECOVER** -- Used to perform complete recovery of the whole database, point-in-time recovery of a database (DBPITR) or tablespace (TSPITR), apply incremental backups to a data file image copy, or recover a corrupt data block or set of data blocks within a data file.
- **VALIDATE** -- Used to check for corrupt blocks and missing files, or to determine whether a backup set can be restored.

Performing Basic Backup and Recovery

Back up and recover a NOARCHIVELOG database

Perform backup and recovery in NOARCHIVELOG mode

When a database is run in NOARCHIVELOG mode, archiving of the redo logs is disabled. The database control file indicates that filled groups are not required to be archived. When a filled group becomes inactive after a log switch, the group is immediately available for reuse by LGWR. A database running in NOARCHIVELOG mode is protected from instance failure but not from media failure. Only the changes made to the database stored in the online redo log groups are available for instance recovery. If a media failure occurs to a database that is in NOARCHIVELOG mode, it is only possible to restore the database to the point of the most recent full database backup.

A full database backup can be either consistent or inconsistent. When a backup is consistent, all read/write data files and control files have the same checkpoint SCN. This ensures that these files contain all changes up to this SCN. A consistent backup does not require recovery after it is restored and it is only possible after a consistent shutdown of the database. A database operating in NOARCHIVELOG mode can only create a valid backup of a consistent database.

If the database has been shut down with the NORMAL, IMMEDIATE, or TRANSACTIONAL options, then it is in a consistent state and you can create a usable backup by copying all of the data files with operating system commands. If the database is open, has just had an instance failure or been SHUTDOWN with the ABORT option, the database is in an inconsistent state. Copying the files at this time will create a backup that is inconsistent with the database SCN. Backups taken for a database in NOARCHIVELOG mode must be consistent. When a database is in ARCHIVELOG mode, it is possible to take inconsistent backups because the archived logs can be used to apply recovery to the datafiles to bring them to a consistent state.

Creating a user-managed consistent whole database backup:

1. Shut down the database with the NORMAL, IMMEDIATE, or TRANSACTIONAL options.

   ```
   SQL> SHUTDOWN IMMEDIATE
   SQL> STARTUP FORCE DBA
   SQL> SHUTDOWN IMMEDIATE
   ```

2. Use an operating system utility to make backups of all data files, all control files, and the initialization parameter file.
3. Restart the database with the STARTUP command.

   ```
   SQL> STARTUP
   ```

Creating a server-managed database backup

To make a consistent database backup using RMAN:

1. Start RMAN and connect to a target database.
2. Shut down the database consistently and then mount it. The following commands will guarantee that the database is in a consistent state for a backup:

```
RMAN> SHUTDOWN IMMEDIATE;
RMAN> STARTUP FORCE DBA;
RMAN> SHUTDOWN IMMEDIATE;
RMAN> STARTUP MOUNT;
```

3. Run the BACKUP DATABASE command. The following command will back up the database to the default backup device:

```
RMAN> BACKUP DATABASE;
```

4. Open the database and resume normal operations. The following command opens the database:

```
RMAN> ALTER DATABASE OPEN;
```

Restoring the database:

When performing a user-managed restore, the DBA is responsible for locating all of the required backup files and placing them in the correct locations. The basic steps to perform a user-managed complete database recovery are:

1. Shut down the database with the NORMAL, IMMEDIATE, or TRANSACTIONAL options.

```
SQL> SHUTDOWN IMMEDIATE
SQL> STARTUP FORCE DBA
SQL> SHUTDOWN IMMEDIATE
```

2. Use an operating system utility to make backups of all data files, all control files, and the initialization parameter file.
3. Restart the database with the STARTUP command.

```
SQL> STARTUP
```

When using RMAN, the RESTORE DATABASE and RECOVER DATABASE commands are used to recover the whole database. In order for the recovery to work, backups of all needed files must exist. The steps below assume that it is possible to restore all data files to their original locations. If the original locations are inaccessible, the SET NEWNAME command must be used to restore them to a different location.

To recover the whole database using RMAN:

1. Place the database in a mounted state. The following command terminates the database instance if it is started and mounts the database.

   ```
   RMAN> STARTUP FORCE MOUNT;
   ```

2. Restore the database. The following command uses the preconfigured disk channel to restore the database.

   ```
   RMAN> RESTORE DATABASE;
   ```

3. Recover the database.

   ```
   RMAN> RECOVER DATABASE;
   ```

4. Open the database.

   ```
   RMAN> ALTER DATABASE OPEN;
   ```

Use SQL in RMAN

It has been possible to execute SQL statement from the RMAN prompt in previous releases by making use of the RMAN 'SQL' command and enclosing the SQL text in double-quotes. For example, the following command archives all unarchived online redo logs:

```
RMAN> SQL "ALTER SYSTEM ARCHIVE LOG CURRENT";
```

In 12c, the SQL command still exists in RMAN, so the above command would work. However, it is now possible to issue most SQL commands from the RMAN prompt without using the SQL keyword. The SQL text also does not need to be enclosed in quotes. The previous example can be executed as follows in 12c:

```
RMAN> ALTER SYSTEM ARCHIVE LOG CURRENT;
```

There are a few commands that exist in both RMAN and SQL but which have very different uses. In these cases, it may be advisable to specify the SQL keyword to eliminate ambiguity. Finally, a DESCRIBE command has been added to RMAN which provides the same functionality as the SQL*Plus DESCRIBE command.

Configuring for Recoverability

Configure and manage RMAN settings

Configure database parameters that affect RMAN operations

The database initialization parameters which have RMAN implications include the following:

- **CONTROL_FILE_RECORD_KEEP_TIME** -- This specifies the minimum number of days before a reusable record in the control file can be reused. The control file contains information used by RMAN for backups and recovery operations. When all available record slots are full, Oracle either expands the control file to make room for a new record or overwrites the oldest record. The CONTROL_FILE_RECORD_KEEP_TIME value should be set to slightly longer than the oldest file that must be kept. For example, if you the whole database is backed up once a week, then the record keep time must be at least 7 days.
- **DB_RECOVERY_FILE_DEST** -- Specifies the default location for the fast recovery area. The fast recovery area contains multiplexed copies of current control files and online redo logs, as well as archived redo logs, flashback logs, and RMAN backups.
- **DB_RECOVERY_FILE_DEST_SIZE** -- Specifies (in bytes) the hard limit on the total space to be used by target database recovery files created in the fast recovery area.
- **LOG_ARCHIVE_DEST_n** -- Defines up to 31 (where n = 1, 2, 3, ...31) destinations, each of which must specify either the LOCATION or the SERVICE attribute to specify where to archive the redo data.
- **DB_CREATE_ONLINE_LOG_DEST_n** -- Specifies the default location for Oracle-managed control files and online redo logs.
- **DB_CREATE_FILE_DEST** -- Specifies the default location for Oracle-managed datafiles. This location is also used as the default location for Oracle-managed control files and online redo logs if none of the DB_CREATE_ONLINE_LOG_DEST_n initialization parameters are specified.

- **DB_UNIQUE_NAME** -- Specifies a globally unique name for the database. For RMAN to work correctly in a Data Guard environment, the DB_UNIQUE_NAME must be unique across all the databases with the same DBID.
- **NLS_DATE_FORMAT** -- Specifies the default date format for the database. It also determines the format used for the time parameters in RMAN commands such as RESTORE, RECOVER, and REPORT.
- **COMPATIBLE** -- Enables you to use a new release of Oracle, while at the same time guaranteeing backward compatibility with an earlier release. In order to make use of unused block compression, the COMPATIBLE initialization parameter must be set to 10.2 or higher.

Configure persistent settings for RMAN

RMAN has a number of different settings to control the specific actions taken during backups. The default settings for most of these parameters make sense for performing standard backup and recovery operations. Understanding what these parameters are will allow you to optimize the behavior for a given database. Persistent settings can be set for each target database, such as backup destinations, device type, and retention policy. The CONFIGURE command allows you to change RMAN current behavior for your backup and recovery environment. If used with the keyword CLEAR, this command will reset the parameter to the default RMAN value. Some examples of the options that can be set follow:

Set the backup retention policy

The following command sets the backup retention policy to maintain three full or level 0 backups of each data file and control file. Any backups older than the third file are considered obsolete. The default value is 1.

```
CONFIGURE RETENTION POLICY TO REDUNDANCY 3;
```

Alternately, the retention policy can be given a recovery window that ensures sufficient backups are kept to recover the database to any point in time back to the supplied value:

```
CONFIGURE RETENTION POLICY TO RECOVERY WINDOW OF 7 DAYS;
```

Set the default device type

When a destination device type is not specific for a backup, RMAN sends it to whatever device type is configured as the default. RMAN is preset to use disk as the default device type. The following command allows you to change the default device type to tape:

```
CONFIGURE DEFAULT DEVICE TYPE TO sbt;
```

Regardless of the default device type, you can specifically direct a backup to a specific device type using the DEVICE TYPE clause of the BACKUP command, as shown in the following examples:

```
BACKUP DEVICE TYPE SBT DATABASE;
BACKUP DEVICE TYPE DISK DATABASE;
```

Configuring Channels

An RMAN channel is a connection to a database server session. The CONFIGURE CHANNEL command is used to configure options for disk or SBT channels. When the CONFIGURE CHANNEL command is used to specify default channel settings for a device, any previous settings are lost. Any settings not specified in the CONFIGURE CHANNEL command will be returned to their default value.

```
CONFIGURE CHANNEL DEVICE TYPE DISK MAXPIECESIZE 1G;
CONFIGURE CHANNEL DEVICE TYPE DISK FORMAT /tmp/%U;
```

Configuring Channels for Disk

RMAN allocates a single disk channel for all operations by default. You can change the default location and format for the file name for that channel. Be aware that when an explicit format is configured for disk channels, RMAN does not create backups by default in the fast recovery area.

```
CONFIGURE CHANNEL DEVICE TYPE DISK FORMAT '/u01/ora_df%t_s%s_s%p';
CONFIGURE CHANNEL DEVICE TYPE DISK FORMAT '+dgroup1';
```

Set the parallelism for a device

When multiple channels are available, RMAN can read or write in parallel. The number of channels should normally match the number of devices available (i.e. three tape drives = three channels). Allocating multiple channels for a single device can negatively affect performance unless your disk subsystem is optimized for multiple channels. The channel parallelism can be set for each device type as follows.

```
CONFIGURE DEVICE TYPE SBT PARALLELISM 2;
```

The command above only affects the parallelism for tape devices and does not alter the values of other device settings not specified.

Configure Control File and Server Parameter File Autobackups

RMAN can be set to automatically back up the control file and server parameter file whenever a backup record is added. In addition, if the database structure metadata in the control file changes and the database is in ARCHIVELOG mode, an autobackup will be taken. Control file autobackup adds additional redundancy to the recovery strategy, allowing RMAN to recover the database even after the loss of the current control file, recovery catalog, and server parameter file. The autobackup feature is enabled and disabled as follows:

```
CONFIGURE CONTROLFILE AUTOBACKUP ON;
CONFIGURE CONTROLFILE AUTOBACKUP OFF;
```

Resetting default values

The RMAN configuration settings can be returned to their default values by using the CLEAR keyword:

```
CONFIGURE DEFAULT DEVICE TYPE CLEAR;
CONFIGURE RETENTION POLICY CLEAR;
CONFIGURE CONTROLFILE AUTOBACKUP CLEAR;
```

View persistent settings

The CONFIGURE command is used to create or change persistent configuration settings that affect RMAN backup, restore, duplication, and maintenance jobs on a particular database. Once created, these settings will be in effect for any RMAN session on this database until explicitly cleared or changed. The SHOW command can be used to display the configurations for one or more databases. The SHOW command can be executed only at the RMAN prompt. In order to perform the SHOW command, one of the following conditions must be met:

- RMAN is connected to a target database, which must be mounted or open.
- RMAN is connected to a recovery catalog and SET DBID must have been run.

Executing SHOW ALL from the RMAN prompt will display all of the RMAN persistent settings. When the settings are at the default value, the results will indicate that by listing '# default' to the right of the configuration setting. For example:

```
RMAN> SHOW ALL;
RMAN configuration parameters for database with db_unique_name OCP1
are:
CONFIGURE RETENTION POLICY TO REDUNDANCY 2;
CONFIGURE BACKUP OPTIMIZATION OFF; # default
CONFIGURE DEFAULT DEVICE TYPE TO DISK; # default
CONFIGURE CONTROLFILE AUTOBACKUP ON;
CONFIGURE CONTROLFILE AUTOBACKUP FORMAT FOR DEVICE TYPE DISK TO
'/u01/oracle/dbs/%F';
CONFIGURE CONTROLFILE AUTOBACKUP FORMAT FOR DEVICE TYPE SBT_TAPE TO
'%F'; # default
CONFIGURE DEVICE TYPE DISK PARALLELISM 1 BACKUP TYPE TO BACKUPSET; #
default
CONFIGURE DEVICE TYPE SBT_TAPE PARALLELISM 1 BACKUP TYPE TO
BACKUPSET; # default
CONFIGURE DATAFILE BACKUP COPIES FOR DEVICE TYPE DISK TO 1; # default
CONFIGURE DATAFILE BACKUP COPIES FOR DEVICE TYPE SBT_TAPE TO 1; #
default
CONFIGURE ARCHIVELOG BACKUP COPIES FOR DEVICE TYPE DISK TO 1; #
default
CONFIGURE ARCHIVELOG BACKUP COPIES FOR DEVICE TYPE SBT_TAPE TO 1; #
default
CONFIGURE CHANNEL DEVICE TYPE 'SBT_TAPE'
PARMS "SBT_LIBRARY=/usr/local/oracle/backup/lib/libobk.so";
CONFIGURE MAXSETSIZE TO UNLIMITED; # default
CONFIGURE ENCRYPTION FOR DATABASE ON;
CONFIGURE ENCRYPTION ALGORITHM 'AES128'; # default
CONFIGURE ARCHIVELOG DELETION POLICY TO NONE; # default
CONFIGURE SNAPSHOT CONTROLFILE NAME TO '/u01/oracle/dbs/cf_snap .f'
```

It is also possible to display the settings individually using the SHOW command. The following example displays only the default device type and channel settings respectively:

```
RMAN> SHOW DEFAULT DEVICE TYPE;
RMAN configuration parameters for database with db_unique_name OCP1
are:
CONFIGURE DEFAULT DEVICE TYPE TO DISK;

RMAN> SHOW CHANNEL;
RMAN configuration parameters for database with db_unique_name OCP1
are:
CONFIGURE CHANNEL DEVICE TYPE 'SBT_TAPE'
PARMS "SBT_LIBRARY=/usr/local/oracle/backup/lib/libobk.so";
```

Information about the RMAN persistent configuration settings can also be found in the view V$RMAN_CONFIGURATION.

- **CONF#** -- A unique key identifying this configuration record within the target database that owns it.
- **NAME** -- The type of configuration.
- **VALUE** -- The CONFIGURE command setting. Example: RETENTION POLICY TO RECOVERY WINDOW OF 10 DAYS
- **CON_ID** -- The ID of the container to which the data pertains.

When a recovery catalog exists, the view RC_RMAN_CONFIGURATION contains information about RMAN persistent configuration settings. It is equivalent to the V$RMAN_CONFIGURATION view.

Specify a retention policy

RMAN retention policies are intended to insure that you have sufficient redundancy in the number of database backups to prevent a catastrophic data loss while keeping you from storing so many that you run out of disk space. The RMAN command CONFIGURE RETENTION POLICY is used to define an automatic backup retention policy. The backup retention policy provides RMAN with the information required to decide if a given backup of datafiles or control files is obsolete. Obsolete backups are no longer needed for recovery. These files can be viewed using the REPORT OBSOLETE command or removed using the DELETE OBSOLETE command.

Even when a retention policy is in place, RMAN will never automatically delete backup files simply because they have become obsolete. The files will remain until removed via the DELETE OBSOLETE command. However, if a database has been configured with a fast recovery area, it is possible that obsolete files can be deleted to satisfy the fast recovery area disk quota rules. If additional space is needed for new files then the database will delete files in the fast recovery area that are either obsolete or have already been backed up to tape. However, the database will not violate the retention policy in order to free up space in the fast recovery area.

Obsolete recovery files should not be confused with expired files. The two have different definitions:

- **Obsolete** -- Backup files are obsolete when according to the current retention policy, they are no longer required for recovery.
- **Expired** -- Backup files are set to expired when an RMAN CROSSCHECK operation is performed and the file cannot be located.

Only control file backups and full or level 0 datafile backups are directly subject to retention policies. If datafiles are part of a backup set, RMAN cannot delete the set until all of the datafile backups within it are obsolete. For individual datafile copies or proxy copies, RMAN can delete them as soon as it is no longer needed according to the policy.

Incremental level 1 backups and archived redo logs become obsolete when no full backups exist that require them. RMAN initially determines which datafile and control file backups are obsolete. All incremental level 1 backups and archived logs that are not required to recover the remaining (non-obsolete) datafile or control file backup are tagged as obsolete. When using a retention policy, backup files should not be removed via non-RMAN utilities. If disk or tape files are removed via OS or media manager commands then this invalidates the ability of RMAN to intelligently control the retention of files.

There are two different types of retention policy. It is only possible to use one of them -- they are mutually exclusive.

- **Recovery Window** -- This is a rolling window of time starting with the present and extending backward in time for a set length. A recovery window defines a point of recoverability, which will be the earliest time from which it is possible to recover following a media failure. If the defined recovery window is two weeks, then RMAN retains full backups and required incremental backups and archived logs that will allow the database to be recovered up to 14 days in the past. A recovery window policy is implemented as follows:

```
CONFIGURE RETENTION POLICY TO RECOVERY WINDOW OF 14 DAYS;
```

- **Backup Redundancy** -- The redundancy retention policy specifies the number backups of each datafile to be retained. When there are more available than the number required, the oldest backups beyond the defined number are obsolete. The default retention policy is configured to REDUNDANCY 1. A backup redundancy of 3 is implemented as follows:

```
CONFIGURE RETENTION POLICY TO REDUNDANCY 3;
```

Configure the Fast Recovery Area

Explain the Fast Recovery Area

The Fast Recovery Area is a location in which the database can store and manage files related to backup and recovery. The location is separate from the database area, where the current database files are located. The fast recovery area can contain control files, online redo logs, archived redo logs, flashback logs, and RMAN backups. A fast recovery area minimizes the need to manually manage disk space for backup related files and balance the use of space among the different types of files. Files in the recovery area are labeled as permanent or transient.

- **Permanent files** -- These are active files used by the database instance. Permanent files that can be in the recovery area include multiplexed copies of the current control file and online redo log files.
- **Transient files** -- These files are not accessed by the database instance and are needed only during recovery operations. Transient files include: archived redo log files, foreign archived redo log files, image copies of datafiles and control files, backup pieces, and flashback logs.

Transient files are generally deleted after they become obsolete or have been backed up to tape. Files placed in the fast recovery area are maintained by Oracle Database and the generated file names use the Oracle Managed Files (OMF) format. When files are no longer needed for recovery, they become eligible for deletion when space for new files is required.

Oracle recommends that archive logs be written to the fast recovery area so that they are automatically managed by the database. Because the fast recovery area is managed by OMF, the generated file names for the archived logs are not determined by the parameter LOG_ARCHIVE_FORMAT. Whether the fast recovery area is used or not, it is always best practice to create multiple copies of archived redo logs.

The following basic options for archiving redo logs are possible, listed in descending order of what Oracle considers to be best practice:

- Enable archiving to the fast recovery area only and use disk mirroring for redundancy. If DB_RECOVERY_FILE_DEST is specified and no LOG_ARCHIVE_DEST_n is specified, then LOG_ARCHIVE_DEST_1 is implicitly set to the recovery area.
- Enable archiving to the fast recovery area and set one or more LOG_ARCHIVE_DEST_n initialization parameters to locations outside the fast recovery area. The fast recovery area can be set as an archiving destination by setting any LOG_ARCHIVE_DEST_n parameter to LOCATION=USE_DB_RECOVERY_FILE_DEST.
- Set LOG_ARCHIVE_DEST_n initialization parameters to archive only to non-fast recovery area locations.

There are several RMAN commands or implicit actions that can create files in the fast recovery area:

- **BACKUP** -- If the FORMAT clause is not specified for disk backups, then RMAN creates backup pieces and image copies in the fast recovery area, with names in Oracle Managed Files (OMF) format.
- **Control File Autobackup** -- RMAN will create control file autobackups in the fast recovery area when no other destination is configured.

- **RESTORE ARCHIVELOG** -- RMAN will restore archived redo log files to the fast recovery area unless the SET ARCHIVELOG DESTINATION is specifically set elsewhere.
- **RECOVER...** -- The RECOVER DATABASE, RECOVER TABLESPACE, and RECOVER ... BLOCK options restore archived redo log files from backup to the recovery area for use during media recovery. RMAN will automatically delete the files after they are applied.
- **FLASHBACK DATABASE** -- As with the RECOVER... options, RMAN will pull any required archived log files to the recovery area and delete them after they have been applied.

Configure the Fast Recovery Area

The following initialization parameters are used to enable the Fast Recovery Area. Only the first two are required, and the database does not require a restart after they have been set.

- **DB_RECOVERY_FILE_DEST_SIZE** -- Specifies the maximum total bytes to be used by the Fast Recovery Area. The basic (minimum) recovery area size should be the sum of all the database files, plus sufficient size for incremental backups and all archive logs that have not been copied to tape. The required size varies widely depending on the backup strategy and whether flashback retention is enabled. This initialization parameter must be specified before DB_RECOVERY_FILE_DEST is enabled.
- **DB_RECOVERY_FILE_DEST** -- Location of the Fast Recovery Area. This can be a directory, file system, or Automatic Storage Management (Oracle ASM) disk group. It cannot be a raw file system.
- **DB_FLASHBACK_RETENTION_TARGET** -- Specifies the upper limit (in minutes) on how far back in time the database may be flashed back. This parameter is required only for Flashback Database.

These parameters cannot be enabled if you have set values for the parameters LOG_ARCHIVE_DEST and LOG_ARCHIVE_DUPLEX_DEST. You must disable those parameters before setting up the Fast Recovery Area. In order to use the Fast Recovery Area, you must instead set values for the LOG_ARCHIVE_DEST_n parameters. Oracle recommends that DB_RECOVERY_FILE_DEST be set to a different value from DB_CREATE_FILE_DEST or any of the DB_CREATE_ONLINE_LOG_DEST_n initialization parameters. A warning will be written to the alert log if DB_RECOVERY_FILE_DEST equals these parameters.

Managing Space in the Fast Recovery Area

The database issues a warning alert when reclaimable space is less than 15% and a critical alert when reclaimable space is less than 3%. An entry is added to the alert log and to the DBA_OUTSTANDING_ALERTS table to warn the DBA of this condition. If not resolved, the database will consume space in the fast recovery area until there is no space left.

You can resolve low space issues in the Fast Recovery Area in several ways:

- Make more disk space available and increase DB_RECOVERY_FILE_DEST_SIZE.
- Move backups from the fast recovery area to tertiary storage such as tape. The BACKUP RECOVERY AREA command will back up all of your recovery area files to tape.
- Run DELETE for any files that have been removed with an operating system utility. The database is not aware of file removed by OS commands.
- Run the RMAN CROSSCHECK command to have RMAN recheck the contents of the fast recovery area and identify expired files, and then use the DELETE EXPIRED command to delete every expired backup from the RMAN repository.
- Delete any unnecessary guaranteed restore points.
- Review your backup retention policy and make it less restrictive.

Information about the Fast Recovery Area is stored in the V$RECOVERY_FILE_DEST dynamic view. In addition, the column IS_RECOVERY_DET_FILE has been added to the following views: V$CONTROLFILE, V$LOGFILE, V$ARCHIVED_LOG, V$DATAFILE_COPY, V$DATAFILE, V$BACKUP_PIECE and the RMAN tables. This column has a value of YES if a file of the corresponding kind has been created in the fast recovery area.

Configure control files and redo log files for recoverability

Multiplex control files

Every Oracle database should have a minimum of two control files whether it is in production or just a development database. Control files are critical to the functioning of the database; the file size is small in comparison to data files; and maintaining multiple copies has a negligible performance impact on the database. Each copy should be stored on a different physical disk. If a control file is damaged or lost due to a disk failure, the associated instance must be shut down. If the control file has been multiplexed, the problem file can be restored using an undamaged copy from another disk and the instance restarted.

When a database has multiplexed control files, the following actions occur:

- Oracle writes to all files listed in the CONTROL_FILES parameter of the database initialization parameter file.
- Oracle reads only the first file listed in the CONTROL_FILES parameter during database operation.
- If any of the control files become unavailable, the instance becomes inoperable and should be aborted.

It is possible to create an additional control file for multiplexing by copying an existing control file to a new location while the database is shut down. The complete process of adding a new multiplexed copy of the current control file is:

1. Shut down the database.
2. Copy an existing control file to a new location, using operating system commands.
3. Edit the CONTROL_FILES parameter in the database initialization parameter file to add the new control file name.
4. Restart the database.

Multiplex redo log files

It is arguably even more important to multiplex redo log groups than the database control file. While both are required for an instance to operate, redo logs are critical to database consistency and the loss of a redo log group is more likely to result in a need for media recovery. As with the control file, multiplexing redo log groups involves creating two or more copies of the redo log files in different locations. The location should ideally be on separate physical disks to eliminate the possibility of a single drive failure destroying all of the copies. When redo log files are multiplexed, LGWR concurrently writes redo log information to each of the multiplexed redo log files.

An Oracle database always has at least two redo log groups. One group is always 'current' and is what the database is currently writing redo log entries to. All other groups are inactive. LGWR never writes concurrently to members of different groups. Each group can be multiplexed with two or more identical copies. These copies provide redundancy that can prevent an unplanned instance shutdown. If LGWR cannot write to the current logfile group, then the instance will shut down immediately. However, if the group is multiplexed and LGWR can write to at least one of the files, then LGWR will ignore the unavailable members and the instance will continue uninterrupted.

As a general rule, multiplexed redo logs should be symmetrical. Each redo log group should have the same number of members, but this is not required. One group could have three multiplexed copies while a second group had only two, and a third only a single file. The only firm requirement is that the database has at least two log groups. Nevertheless, the best practice is to multiplex all groups to the same level.

It is possible to create new redo log members for an existing group with the SQL statement ALTER DATABASE with the ADD LOGFILE MEMBER clause. The following example adds a new member to redo log group number 2:

```
ALTER DATABASE ADD LOGFILE MEMBER '/oracle/dbs/log2b.rdo' TO GROUP 2;
```

The size of the new redo log file is determined from the size of the existing members of the group. An alternate syntax to perform the same task is to identify the target group by specifying all of the other group members of the group in the TO clause:

```
ALTER DATABASE ADD LOGFILE MEMBER '/oracle/dbs/log2c.rdo'
TO ('/oracle/dbs/log2a.rdo', '/oracle/dbs/log2b.rdo');
```

Using the RMAN Recovery Catalog

Create and use an RMAN Recovery Catalog

Configure a recovery catalog

The RMAN recovery catalog is a database schema in an Oracle database that is used to store metadata about one or more Oracle databases. The data from this schema is used by RMAN when performing recovery operations. While the catalog can be stored in a database used for other purposes, it is generally stored in a dedicated database. The catalog stores information about RMAN operations for all of the target databases that have been registered in it. Any time that RMAN is connected to a recovery catalog, all metadata will be pulled exclusively from the catalog instead of the control file. By centralizing the metadata for multiple target databases, the recovery catalog makes reporting and administration easier. A recovery catalog includes the following information:

- Datafile and archived redo log backup sets and backup pieces
- Datafile copies
- Archived redo logs and their copies
- Database structure (tablespaces and datafiles)
- Stored scripts, which are named user-created sequences of RMAN commands
- Persistent RMAN configuration settings

Recovery catalogs are required in the following cases:

- **Loss of control files** -- If the current control file and all backups are lost for a given database, a recovery catalog is required. Recovery catalogs contain the same metadata as the RMAN repository stored in the control file of each target database.
- **Recovery from very old backup** -- The control file contains a more limited amount of history than a recovery catalog. If you need to perform a recovery from a backup that goes back further in time

than is stored in the control file, then a recovery catalog is required.

- **RMAN Scripts** -- RMAN scripts can be stored in a recovery catalog. The scripts are then available to every RMAN client that can connect to the target database and recovery catalog. By contrast, command files are only available if the RMAN client has access to the file system on which they are stored.
- **Data Guard** -- If you want to use RMAN in a Data Guard environment, a recovery catalog is required. The recovery catalog stores RMAN metadata for all primary and standby databases.

Before creating a recovery catalog, you must determine what database to put it in and what schema to use. You should not put the catalog in a database that will itself be a target of the catalog. Using a dedicated catalog database is the normal and suggested option. In addition, the catalog database should not be on the same hard drive as any of its target databases or a single hard drive failure can take out both the target database and the catalog required to recover the target. The greater the independence between the catalog and target databases, the more robust the recovery scenario becomes. Once a database is selected, the catalog will be stored in a schema on that database (which cannot be SYS).

The space required by the catalog schema depends primarily on the number of databases that will be targets of the catalog. The size will also increase as the number of backups and archived log files for each individual database grows. RMAN scripts stored in the catalog will use space as well. The Oracle Database Backup and Recovery User's Guide contains more information and formulas on estimating size requirements.

Once a catalog database and schema have been determined and sufficient space exists in the catalog tablespace, you can create the schema owner and grant the schema all of the privileges required. In the example below, a dedicated database (catdb) with a tablespace called RMANCAT_TS exists. The SYS user has connected to catdb with SYSDBA privileges.

To create the recovery catalog schema and set up the default and temporary tablespaces:

```
SQL>  CREATE USER recodude IDENTIFIED BY [password]
      TEMPORARY TABLESPACE temp
      DEFAULT TABLESPACE rmancat_ts
      QUOTA UNLIMITED ON rmancat_ts;
```

Grant the RECOVERY_CATALOG_OWNER role to the rman schema.

```
SQL> GRANT RECOVERY_CATALOG_OWNER TO recodude;
```

Once the catalog schema exists, the RMAN CREATE CATALOG command is used to create the catalog tables in the default tablespace of the catalog owner. To create the recovery catalog you must start RMAN and connect to the catalog database as the recovery catalog owner. Once connected, run the CREATE CATALOG command to create the catalog. This can take several minutes.

```
RMAN> CREATE CATALOG;
```

You can specify the tablespace name for the catalog in the CREATE CATALOG command to store it in a tablespace other than the default for the schema:

```
RMAN> CREATE CATALOG TABLESPACE users;
```

Register target databases in a recovery catalog

Once a catalog exists, you must register the target databases in the catalog. Until a database has been registered, RMAN cannot store any metadata about backup operations in the catalog. Unregistered databases will continue to use the control file as their sole source of RMAN metadata during backup and recovery operations. To register a new target database, you must:

Start RMAN and connect to both the target database and to the recovery catalog. The database containing the recovery catalog must be open and the target database must be mounted.

```
% rman TARGET / CATALOG recodude@catdb
```

Register the target database in the connected recovery catalog via the REGISTER DATABASE command:

```
REGISTER DATABASE;
```

RMAN will add information about the target database to the appropriate catalog tables. It then copies information from the control file of the target database into the catalog to synchronize the catalog with the control file. Once the command has completed, you can verify that the registration was successful by running the REPORT SCHEMA command:

```
REPORT SCHEMA;

Report of database schema
File Size(MB)    Tablespace       RB segs Datafile Name
---- ---------- ---------------- ------- -------------------
1        327680 SYSTEM           NO      /u01/oradata/system01.dbf
2         30720 UNDOTBS          YES     /u01/oradata/undotbs01.dbf
3         20480 INDEX_TS         NO      /u01/oradata/index_ts01.dbf
4         10240 TOOLS_TS         NO      /u01/oradata/tools_ts01.dbf
5         20480 USER_TS          NO      /u01/oradata/user_ts01.dbf
```

Catalog additional backup files

When you first create the recovery catalog, it is possible that you have datafile copies, backup pieces, or archived logs on disk that have aged out of the control file. It is possible to add them to the recovery catalog with the CATALOG command. Doing this allows RMAN to make use of the older backups during restore operations. The following commands can be used to add files to the catalog:

- **CATALOG DATAFILECOPY** -- Allows you to add a data file backup to the catalog.
- **CATALOG ARCHIVELOG** -- Allows you to add one or more archived log files to the catalog.
- **CATALOG BACKUPPIECE** -- Allows you to add a backup piece to the catalog.
- **CATALOG START WITH** -- Allows you to add multiple files from a given directory to the catalog. RMAN will list the files to be added to the RMAN repository and prompts for confirmation before adding the backups.

When using the CATALOG START WITH command, you should be aware that if multiple directory paths contain the text supplied, you may catalog files that you did not intend to. Consider a file system that has one directory called **/u01/backups** and another called **/u01/backups/old** that contain backup files. Issuing the following command catalogs all files in both directories:

```
CATALOG START WITH '/u01/backups';
```

To catalog only backups in the /u01/backups directory, the correct command should be:

```
CATALOG START WITH '/u01/backups/';
```

Resynchronize a recovery catalog

Synchronizing the recovery catalog is the process of comparing the recovery catalog to the control file (either the current file or a backup) and updating the catalog with any metadata that has been changed or is not present on the catalog. RMAN automatically resynchronizes the catalog when most commands are issued, so long as the target control file is mounted and the catalog is available. It is possible to perform a full or a partial resynchronization of the catalog.

- **Partial** -- During a partial resynchronization, RMAN will update changed metadata about new backups, new archived redo logs, and so on from the target control file. Metadata in the catalog about the database physical schema will not be updated.
- **Full** -- In a full resynchronization, RMAN will locate and update all changed metadata records, including those for the database schema. A full resynchronization is performed only after structural changes have been made to the database (such as changes to database files) or if the RMAN persistent configuration has been altered.

During a full resynchronization, RMAN will create a temporary backup called a snapshot control file. This file is used to ensure that RMAN has a consistent view of the control file. It is intended only to be used for a short period of time and is not registered in the catalog. The control file checkpoint is maintained in the recovery catalog to verify the catalog currency.

If RMAN is connected to the target database and the recovery catalog, it will automatically resynchronize the recovery catalog whenever commands are executed. You should seldom need to manually resynchronize the catalog. However, there are times when it is required:

- **Catalog Unavailability** -- If you issue RMAN commands at a time when the recovery catalog is unavailable, you should open the catalog database later and use the RESYNC CATALOG command to resynchronize it manually. This might be the case if your target database and catalog database are in different locations and the availability of both at the same time cannot be guaranteed.
- **Infrequent Backups** -- If a target database running in ARCHIVELOG mode is backed up infrequently, it possible that a significant number of redo logs are archived between database backups. The recovery catalog is not updated automatically when a redo log switch occurs or when a redo log is archived. Metadata about redo log switches and archived redo logs is stored only in the control file. When RMAN backup operations are infrequent, you should regularly issue a RESYNC CATALOG to ensure this information is stored in the recovery catalog.

- **Standby Database** -- It is possible to create or alter the RMAN configuration for a standby database while not connected to the database as TARGET. After doing so, to update the control file of the standby database you can resynchronize the standby database manually.
- **Prevent Loss of Metadata** -- The data in the recovery catalog originates from the control file and the data in the control file is only kept for a limited time before being overwritten. You must ensure that the catalog is synchronized with the control file before uncataloged metadata gets overwritten. The initialization parameter CONTROL_FILE_RECORD_KEEP_TIME sets the minimum number of days that records are guaranteed to be kept in the control file. The catalog must be resynchronized at intervals less than that value by either performing backup operations that implicitly resynchronize the catalog or performing manual resynchronizations.

The RESYNC CATALOG command forces a full resynchronization of the recovery catalog. The steps to perform this are:

- Start RMAN and connect to a target database and recovery catalog.
- Mount or open the target database if it is not already mounted or open via the STARTUP MOUNT command.
- Resynchronize the recovery catalog using the RESYNC CATALOG command at the RMAN prompt.

Use and maintain RMAN stored scripts

RMAN recovery catalogs allow for the creation of stored scripts. Stored scripts act much like RMAN command files. However, command files require access to the file system where they are saved, whereas stored scripts require only a connection to the catalog. The CREATE SCRIPT command is used to create a stored script in the recovery catalog. It allows you to create a named sequence of RMAN commands in the recovery catalog for later execution. The CREATE SCRIPT command can only be executed from the RMAN prompt while connected to a target database and an open recovery catalog. Stored scripts can be either Global or Local:

- **GLOBAL** -- A global script is available for use with any database registered in the recovery catalog. Global scripts are available to virtual private catalogs with read-only access. It is only possible to create or update global scripts while connected to the base recovery catalog.
- **LOCAL** -- Local scripts created for the current target database only. They are not available to virtual private catalogs.

Local and Global scripts have different namespaces. It is possible to have a local and a global script of the same name. It is not possible to have two global scripts of the same name or two local scripts of the same name for a given target database.

Stored scripts can make use of substitution variables. &1 indicates where to place the first value, &2 indicate where to place the second value, and so on. If any special characters are included, they must be quoted. The syntax for substitution variables is &integer followed by an optional period. When the substitution variable is parsed, the optional period is replaced with the value. This allows the substitution text to be followed by another integer. In the following three cases, the value **orcl_backup** is passed:

- &1 -> orcl_backup
- &1.1 -> orcl_backup1
- &1..1 -> orcl_backup.1

Stored scripts with substitution variables must be provided with example values at create time. These values can be provided explicitly with the USING clause when starting RMAN or they can be entered when prompted.

Create a Local Stored Script

After starting RMAN, connect to the target database as TARGET, and connect to a recovery catalog. The following steps create a stored script called full_backup and then run it:

```
RMAN> CONNECT TARGET SYS@oraprod

target database Password: [password]
connected to target database: PROD (DBID=38752058)

RMAN> CONNECT CATALOG recodude@catdb

recovery catalog database Password: [password]
connected to recovery catalog database

RMAN> CREATE SCRIPT full_backup
COMMENT "Perform full backup of database and archive logs"
{
    BACKUP
      INCREMENTAL LEVEL 0 TAG full_backup
      FORMAT "/u02/backup/%U"
      DATABASE PLUS ARCHIVELOG;
}

RMAN> RUN { EXECUTE SCRIPT full_backup; }
```

Create a Global Stored Script

This example creates a global script that backs up the database and archived redo log files:

```
RMAN> CONNECT TARGET SYS@oraprod

target database Password: [password]
connected to target database: ORAPROD (DBID=38752058)

RMAN> CONNECT CATALOG recoman@catdb

recovery catalog database Password: [password]
connected to recovery catalog database

RMAN> CREATE GLOBAL SCRIPT global_full_backup
     { BACKUP DATABASE PLUS ARCHIVELOG; }
```

This script can now be accessed while connected to a different database:

```
RMAN> CONNECT TARGET SYS@oradev

target database Password: [password]
connected to target database: ORADEV (DBID=39823641)

RMAN> CONNECT CATALOG recoman@catdb

recovery catalog database Password: [password]
connected to recovery catalog database

RMAN> RUN { EXECUTE SCRIPT global_full_backup; }
```

Create a Stored Script with Substitution Variables

The following example creates a backup script that includes three substitution variables. As the last step in creating the script, RMAN prompts for initial values for the substitution variables.

```
RMAN> CONNECT TARGET /
RMAN> CONNECT CATALOG recoman@catdb

recovery catalog database Password: [password]
connected to recovery catalog database

RMAN> CREATE SCRIPT datafile_backup
2> { BACKUP DATAFILE &1 TAG &2 FORMAT '/u01/&3_%U'; }
Enter value for 1: 1

Enter value for 2: dfile1_bkup

Enter value for 3: dfile1

created script datafile_backup
```

When the script is executed, it is possible to pass different values to it:

```
RMAN> RUN { EXECUTE SCRIPT backup_df USING 2 dfile2_bkup dfile2; }
```

After the values are substituted, the script executes as follows:

```
BACKUP DATAFILE 2 TAG dfile2_bkup FORMAT '/u01/dfile2_%U';
```

Deleting a stored script

You can delete stored scripts with the DELETE SCRIPT command. The following example deletes the global script named global_full_backup:

```
RMAN> DELETE GLOBAL SCRIPT global_full_backup;

deleted global script: global_full_backup
```

Replacing an Existing Script

You can overwrite an existing stored script using the REPLACE SCRIPT command. The following example shows how to replace an existing script:

```
RMAN> CONNECT TARGET SYS@oraprod

target database Password: [password]
connected to target database: ORAPROD (DBID=38752058)

RMAN> CONNECT CATALOG recoman@catdb

recovery catalog database Password: [password]
connected to recovery catalog database

RMAN> CREATE SCRIPT full_backup
COMMENT "Perform full backup of database and archive logs"
{
    BACKUP
      INCREMENTAL LEVEL 0 TAG full_backup
      FORMAT "/u02/backup/%U"
      DATABASE;
}
```

The LIST SCRIPT NAMES command will list all scripts known to the recovery catalog:

```
RMAN> LIST SCRIPT NAMES;
```

```
List of Stored Scripts in Recovery Catalog


    Scripts of Target Database ORAPROD


       Script Name
       Description
       ------------------------------------------------
       full_backup
       Perform full backup of database and archive logs

       datafile_backup
```

However -- the script description is incorrect. As created, it does not back up the archive logs. You can replace the script with the following command:

```
RMAN> REPLACE SCRIPT full_backup
COMMENT "Perform full backup of database and archive logs"
{
    BACKUP
      INCREMENTAL LEVEL 0 TAG full_backup
      FORMAT "/u02/backup/%U"
      DATABASE PLUS ARCHIVELOG;
}
replaced script full_backup
```

Note that if you are replacing a Global script, you must use the REPLACE GLOBAL SCRIPT command.

Viewing stored scripts

The PRINT SCRIPT command allows you to see what actions are performed by a stored script:

```
RMAN> PRINT SCRIPT full_backup;

printing stored script: full_backup
 { BACKUP
      INCREMENTAL LEVEL 0 TAG full_backup
      FORMAT "/u02/backup/%U"
      DATABASE PLUS ARCHIVELOG;
}
```

Upgrade and drop a recovery catalog

Upgrading a Recovery Catalog

If your RMAN client requires a version of the recovery catalog schema that is newer than what you currently have installed, then you must upgrade the catalog. It is possible to use the compatibility matrix in the Oracle Database Backup and Recovery Reference to determine which schema versions are compatible with which versions of RMAN. If the recovery catalog is at a version greater than what is required by the RMAN client and you issue the UPGRADE CATALOG command, an error will be generated. However, even if the recovery catalog is current and does not require upgrading, it is possible to issue the UPGRADE CATALOG command. This allows you to re-create the catalog packages at any time.

Before attempting to upgrade the catalog, you should determine what the current version is. The schema version of the recovery catalog is stored in the recovery catalog itself. To determine the version of the recovery catalog, query the RCVER view:

1. Start SQL*Plus and connect to the recovery catalog database as the catalog owner.
2. Query the RCVER table to obtain the schema version:

```
SELECT *
FROM   rcver;

VERSION
------------
09.00.01
```

If the query returns multiple rows, it means that the catalog has been upgrade since it was first installed. The highest version in the RCVER table is the current catalog schema version. The steps to upgrade the recovery catalog are:

1. If you created the recovery catalog owner in a release before 10gR1, and if the RECOVERY_CATALOG_OWNER role did not include the CREATE TYPE privilege, then grant it.

```
SQL> GRANT CREATE TYPE TO rman;
SQL> EXIT;
```

2. Start RMAN and connect RMAN to the recovery catalog database.
3. Run the UPGRADE CATALOG command:

```
RMAN> UPGRADE CATALOG;
recovery catalog owner is rman
enter UPGRADE CATALOG command again to confirm catalog
upgrade
```

4. Run the UPDATE CATALOG command again to confirm:

```
RMAN> UPGRADE CATALOG;
recovery catalog upgraded to version 12.01.00
DBMS_RCVMAN package upgraded to version 12.01.00
DBMS_RCVCAT package upgraded to version 12.01.00
```

Dropping a Recovery Catalog

The RMAN DROP CATALOG command will remove the objects that were created by the CREATE CATALOG command. If any objects in the schema exist that were <u>not</u> created by CREATE CATALOG, these will not be removed by the DROP CATALOG command. When a recovery catalog is dropped and there are no backups of the recovery catalog schema, backups of all target databases registered in the dropped catalog may become unusable. The DROP CATALOG command cannot be used to unregister a single database from a recovery catalog that has multiple target databases registered. The command will delete the recovery catalog record of backups for all target databases registered in the catalog. The steps to drop a recovery catalog schema are:

1. Start RMAN and connect to a target database and recovery catalog. Connect to the recovery catalog as the owner of the catalog schema to be dropped.

```
% rman TARGET / CATALOG rmandude@catdb
```

2. Run the DROP CATALOG command:

```
DROP CATALOG;
recovery catalog owner is rmandude
enter DROP CATALOG command again to confirm catalog removal
```

3. Run the DROP CATALOG command again to confirm:

```
DROP CATALOG;
```

Protect the RMAN Recovery Catalog

Back up the recovery catalog

When creating a backup strategy, you must be sure that it includes backing up the recovery catalog database. If a hardware failure destroys the database holding your recovery catalog, this will lose the metadata for all of your target databases. Losing the metadata will make any recovery of those databases considerably more difficult. The recovery catalog database should be backed up as often as the target databases. As a general rule, the recovery catalog should be backed up on the same schedule as your target databases and after the last has completed. For example, if you have three databases being backed up each week, one each Thursday, Friday, and Saturday, then back up the recovery catalog database on Sunday. Having a backup of the recovery catalog will be useful in a disaster recovery scenario. In a situation where you have to restore the recovery catalog database, the record of backups in the restored recovery catalog database will allow you to restore any of the three target databases.

RMAN can be used to make the backups for the recovery catalog database. However, since you will be backing up the catalog itself, start RMAN with the NOCATALOG option so that RMAN will use the control file of the catalog database for the metadata repository. The following guidelines should be used for a recovery catalog backup strategy:

- The recovery catalog database should always be run in ARCHIVELOG mode.
- The retention policy should be set to a REDUNDANCY value greater than 1.
- Use two separate media to back up the database (i.e. disk and tape).
- Execute BACKUP DATABASE PLUS ARCHIVELOG at regular intervals.
- Use the control file rather than another recovery catalog as the metadata repository.
- Configure the control file autobackup feature to ON.

Re-create an unrecoverable recovery catalog

A recovery catalog is composed of data in an Oracle database like any other schema. If it has been backed up, then it should be possible to restore and recover it as you would any other database with RMAN. However, if it is not possible to restore the recovery catalog database through standard Oracle recovery procedures, the catalog must be recreated. This might happen if the recovery catalog database has never been backed up or it has been backed up but the data file backups or archived logs are not available.

It is possible to partially re-creating the contents of the missing recovery catalog using the following two options:

- **RESYNC CATALOG** -- This command can be used to update the recovery catalog with any RMAN repository information from the control file of the target database or a control file copy. This will not be able to restore any metadata from records that have been aged out of the control file.
- **CATALOG START WITH** -- This command can be used to recatalog any available backups.

Export and import the recovery catalog

It is possible to export a recovery catalog from one database and import it back into a second database. An export can also serve as a logical backup to help prevent the loss of data in the event of a media failure. The following steps can be used to export a recovery catalog from one database and import it into another.

1. Use one of the Oracle Export utilities to export the catalog data from the database.
2. Create a recovery catalog user on the database you are exporting to and grant the user necessary privileges.
3. Use the corresponding Import utility to import the catalog data into the recovery catalog user schema.

The CREATE CATALOG command should not be issued against the new database either before or after importing the catalog into the database. The import operation will create the catalog in the second database.

Implementing Backup Strategies

Use various RMAN backup types and strategies

Enable ARCHIVELOG mode

In order to toggle the archiving mode of the database, use the ALTER DATABASE statement with the ARCHIVELOG or NOARCHIVELOG clause. You must be logged in to the database with administrator privileges in order to alter the archiving mode. The following steps will enable ARCHIVELOG on a database:

1. Shut down the database instance. The database must be closed and all associated instances shut down in order to switch the database archiving mode. It is also not possible to change the mode from ARCHIVELOG to NOARCHIVELOG if any datafiles need media recovery.
2. Edit the initialization parameter file. Add required parameters to specify the destinations for the archived redo log files.
3. Perform a STARTUP MOUNT on the database.
4. Change the database archiving mode by issuing ALTER DATABASE ARCHIVELOG.
5. Open the database for normal operations by issuing ALTER DATABASE OPEN.
6. Shut down the database.
7. Back up the database. Because changing the archiving mode updates the control file, you must back up all of your database files and control file. Previous backups are no longer usable.

Create tape and disk based backups

When a backup command is issued but no destination device type is specified, it will be directed to the configured default device. RMAN is preconfigured to use disk as the default device type. It may be necessary to alter the default device type from disk to tape, or change it back from tape to disk. The commands to change the default device types are:

- **CONFIGURE DEFAULT DEVICE TYPE TO DISK** -- This specifies that backups go to disk by default. When a recovery area is enabled, then the backup location defaults to the fast recovery area. Otherwise, the backup location defaults to an operating system-specific directory on disk.
- **CONFIGURE DEFAULT DEVICE TYPE TO sbt** -- Specifies that backups go to tape by default. For this to work, RMAN must be set up for use with a media manager. Once this has been done, it is possible to configure RMAN to make backups to tape and specify SBT as the default device type.

The default device type can be overridden by using the DEVICE TYPE clause of the BACKUP command:

```
BACKUP DEVICE TYPE sbt DATABASE;
BACKUP DEVICE TYPE DISK DATABASE;
```

To change the configured default device type:

1. Start RMAN and connect to a target database and a recovery catalog (if used).
2. Run the SHOW ALL command to show the currently configured default device.
3. Run the CONFIGURE DEFAULT DEVICE TYPE command, specifying either TO DISK or TO sbt.

Create whole database backups

A whole database backup includes a backup of the control file and all data files that belong to a database. When a database has archiving enabled, a whole database backup can be made with the database mounted or open. The RMAN command BACKUP DATABASE can be used to perform a whole database backup.

```
BACKUP DATABASE;
```

Adding the PLUS ARCHIVELOGS clause will back up the database, switch the online redo logs, and include archived logs in the backup. This guarantees that you have the full set of archived logs through the time of the backup and guarantees that you can perform media recovery after restoring this backup.

```
BACKUP DATABASE PLUS ARCHIVELOG;
```

It is also possible to create a whole database backup using OS commands or a third party backup utility. When using OS commands, tablespaces being backed up must be placed into backup mode.

Create consistent and inconsistent backups

To make a consistent database backup using RMAN, the database must have been shut down cleanly. The following steps will make a consistent backup:

5. Start RMAN and connect to a target database.
6. Shut down the database consistently and then mount it. The following commands will guarantee that the database is in a consistent state for a backup:

```
RMAN> SHUTDOWN IMMEDIATE;
RMAN> STARTUP FORCE DBA;
RMAN> SHUTDOWN IMMEDIATE;
RMAN> STARTUP MOUNT;
```

7. Run the BACKUP DATABASE command. The following command will back up the database to the default backup device:

```
RMAN> BACKUP DATABASE;
```

8. Open the database and resume normal operations. The following command opens the database:

```
RMAN> ALTER DATABASE OPEN;
```

Inconsistent database backups are created while the database is running. Technically they could also be made when the database has not been shut down cleanly, but it is difficult to imagine why anyone would do that. The database must be running in ARCHIVELOG mode for an inconsistent backup to be usable for recovery. The following steps will make an inconsistent backup of a running database:

1. Start RMAN and connect to a target database.
2. Run the BACKUP DATABASE command. The following command will back up the database to the default backup device:

```
RMAN> BACKUP DATABASE;
```

The RESTORE DATABASE and RECOVER DATABASE commands are used to recover the whole database. In order for the recovery to work, backups of all needed files must exist. The steps below assume that it is possible to restore all data files to their original locations. If the original locations are inaccessible, the SET NEWNAME command must be used to restore them to a different location.

To recover the whole database using RMAN:

5. Place the database in a mounted state. The following command terminates the database instance if it is started and mounts the database.

```
RMAN> STARTUP FORCE MOUNT;
```

6. Restore the database. The following command uses the preconfigured disk channel to restore the database.

```
RMAN> RESTORE DATABASE;
```

7. Recover the database.

```
RMAN> RECOVER DATABASE;
```

8. Open the database.

```
RMAN> ALTER DATABASE OPEN;
```

Create backup sets and image copies

When backing up to disk, RMAN can be configured to create either backup sets or image copies by default. Backups to tape devices can only be a backup set. Backup sets contain one or more data files, control files, server parameter files, and archived redo log files. Each binary file in a backup set is referred to as a backup piece. The contents of a backup set are divided among multiple backup pieces only if the backup piece size is limited using MAXPIECESIZE. This keyword is an option of the ALLOCATE CHANNEL or CONFIGURE CHANNEL command. Backup sets are written in a proprietary format that can only be created or restored using RMAN. The default RMAN backup type for disk is an uncompressed backup set. This is the equivalent of performing the following configure command:

```
CONFIGURE DEVICE TYPE DISK BACKUP TYPE TO BACKUPSET;
```

Unless the configure command has been used to set the default backup type to COPY, all RMAN backups will use backup sets unless explicitly set otherwise. On a database where the default has been set to COPY, the following command overrides the default with the AS BACKUPSET clause of the BACKUP command:

```
BACKUP AS BACKUPSET
  DEVICE TYPE DISK
  DATABASE;
```

When RMAN creates image copies, the result is bit-for-bit copies of each data file, archived redo log file, or control file. Images copies can be used as-is to perform recovery. They are generated with the RMAN BACKUP AS COPY command, an operating system command such as the UNIX cp, or by the Oracle archiver process. The default RMAN backup type can be set to image using the CONFIGURE DEVICE TYPE COMMAND:

```
CONFIGURE DEVICE TYPE DISK BACKUP TYPE TO COPY;
```

It is also possible to override the default with the AS COPY clause of the BACKUP command:

```
BACKUP AS COPY
  DEVICE TYPE DISK
  DATABASE;
```

Create backups of read-only tablespaces

When a tablespace has been marked as read-only, it is possible to simply back up the online data files. There is no requirement to place the tablespace in backup mode because the database does not permit changes to the data files. To back up online read-only tablespaces in an open database:

1. Query the DBA_TABLESPACES view to determine which tablespaces are read-only.

    ```
    SELECT tablespace_name
    FROM   dba_tablespaces
    WHERE  status = 'READ ONLY';
    ```

2. Identify all of the tablespace's data files by querying the DBA_DATA_FILES data dictionary view.

    ```
    SELECT file_name
    FROM   sys.dba_data_files
    WHERE  tablespace_name = 'ARCHIVE_RO';

    FILE_NAME
    -------------------------------------------
    /u01/oradata/ocp1/archive01.dbf
    /u01/oradata/ocp1/archive02.dbf
    ```

3. Back up the online data files of the read-only tablespace with operating system commands. There is no need to take the tablespace offline or put the tablespace in backup mode:

    ```
    % cp $ORACLE_HOME/oradata/ocp1/archive*.dbf /u02/backup/
    ```

4. Optionally, export the metadata in the read-only tablespace. By using the transportable tablespace feature, you can quickly restore the data files and import the metadata in case of media failure or user error.

```
% expdp DIRECTORY=dpump_dir1 DUMPFILE=archive.dmp
TRANSPORT_TABLESPACES=archive_ro LOGFILE=tts.log
```

Employ best practices for data warehouse backups

By their nature, data warehouses can consist of enormous amounts of data -- potentially hundreds of terabytes. Creating a feasible backup and recovery strategy for them is critical to avoid the potential for losing data. Oracle has suggested several best practices for implementing a backup and recovery strategy for a data warehouse.

- **Use ARCHIVELOG Mode** -- It is difficult to imagine any production database not being run in archivelog mode. Archived redo logs are crucial for recovery when no data can be lost, because they constitute a record of changes to the database. Archivelog mode provides considerably more recovery options that are possible with noarchivelog mode.
- **Use RMAN** -- RMAN has numerous advantages over user-managed backups. Some of the reasons for integrating RMAN into the backup and recovery strategy for a data warehouse include: extensive reporting, incremental backups, downtime free backups, backup and restore validation, backup and restore optimization, easily integrates with media managers, block media recovery, archive log validation and management, and corrupt block detection.
- **Use Read-Only Tablespaces** -- The size of a typical data warehouse can mean that backups take several hours. Minimizing the amount of data to be backed up can significantly improve the overall backup performance. Read-only tablespaces are an easy way to reduce the amount of data to be backed up in a data warehouse. A read-only tablespace only need to be backed up once (possibly more than once for redundancy).

- **Plan for NOLOGGING Operations** -- Data warehouses often execute bulk-data operations using the NOLOGGING mode. When an operation runs in NOLOGGING mode, no data is written to the redo log. However, since the data to support recovery is written to the log file during NOLOGGING operations, this has implications for the backup strategy. Database backup operations should never take place when a NOLOGGING operation is occurring. Oracle does not enforce this, so the DBA is responsible for scheduling the backup jobs so that they do not overlap NOLOGGING operations.
- **Not All Tablespaces are Equally Important** -- DBAs can create more efficient backup and recovery strategies that take into account how important tablespaces are in their warehouse. For example, there may be tablespaces that are dedicated to scratch space for end-users to store temporary tables and incremental results. It is possible that these tablespaces may not need to be backed up and restored. In the event that these tablespaces are lost, end users would need to re-create their own data objects. Whether this type of optimization can be made depends entirely upon the use of the data warehouse in question.

Performing Backups

Perform full and incremental backups

Create full and incremental backups

The RMAN BACKUP INCREMENTAL command creates an incremental backup of a database. Incremental backups capture block-level changes to a database made after a previous incremental backup. Recovery with incremental backups is faster than using redo logs alone. There are three types of incremental backups:

- **Level 0** -- This is the starting point for an incremental backup. It backs up all blocks in the database and is identical in content to a full backup.
- **Level 1 Differential** -- This backup contains only blocks changed since the most recent incremental backup. This is the default Level 1 backup.
- **Level 1 Cumulative** -- This backup contains only blocks changed since the most recent level 0 backup.

When restoring incremental backups, RMAN uses the level 0 backup as the starting point. It then uses the level 1 backups to update changed blocks where possible to avoid reapplying changes from redo one at a time. If incremental backups are available, then RMAN uses them during recovery.

The following example creates a level 0 incremental backup to serve as a base for an incremental backup strategy:

```
BACKUP INCREMENTAL LEVEL 0 DATABASE;
```

The following example creates a level 1 cumulative incremental backup:

```
BACKUP INCREMENTAL LEVEL 1 CUMULATIVE DATABASE;
```

The following example creates a level 1 differential incremental backup:

```
BACKUP INCREMENTAL LEVEL 1 DATABASE;
```

Use the Oracle-suggested backup strategy

Oracle's suggested backup strategy is a scheduled disk backup that provides efficient recoverability to any point in a specified recovery window. It makes use of incrementally updated backups to provide improved performance over full-database backups. This strategy requires an initial image copy of each data file. It then rolls forward the image copies daily by applying an incremental level 1 backup.

In order to use the Oracle suggested backup strategy, the following requirements must be met:

- The database must be in ARCHIVELOG mode.
- A fast recovery area must exist, or a default device for storing backups be configured.
- A database host user must be added to the OSBACKUPDBA operating system group.

For each data file, the strategy calls for the following:

- On day 1 of the strategy, RMAN creates an incremental level 0 image copy. This contains the data file contents at the beginning of day 1.
- On day 2, RMAN creates a differential incremental level 1 backup that contains the blocks changed during day 1.
- On day n for day 3 and onward, RMAN applies the level 1 backup from the beginning of day n-1 to the level 0 backup. This action brings the data file copy to its state at the beginning of day n-1. RMAN then creates a new level 1 backup that contains the blocks changed during day n-1.

In the event that recovery is required, RMAN can apply this incremental level 1 backup to the data file rolled forward on day n-1 to the beginning of day n. RMAN can use archived redo log files to recover the database to any point during day n.

The following script implements the Oracle suggested backup strategy in a Linux environment. The script can be used to back up a non-CDB or a whole multitenant container database (CDB). Once the script exists, a crontab file should be created to run it every day well before business hours (for example 2 A.M.).

```
#!/bin/sh
export ORACLE_HOME=/u01/app/oracle/product/11.2.0/dbhome_1
export ORACLE_SID=orcl
PATH=$ORACLE_HOME/bin:$PATH
rman <<EOF
connect target /
RUN {
 ALLOCATE CHANNEL disk_iub DEVICE TYPE DISK;
 RECOVER COPY OF DATABASE WITH TAG daily_iub;
 BACKUP INCREMENTAL LEVEL 1 FOR RECOVER OF COPY WITH TAG daily_iub
DATABASE;
}
exit
EOF
```

Manage backups

Configure and monitor block change tracking

The block change tracking feature improves backup performance for incremental backups by recording changed blocks for each data file. If block change tracking is enabled, RMAN uses a block change tracking file to identify changed blocks during incremental backups. This file keeps RMAN from having to scan every block in the data file that it is backing up. Block change tracking is disabled by default. A single block change tracking file is created for the whole database. By default, the change tracking file is created as an Oracle managed file in the destination specified by the DB_CREATE_FILE_DEST initialization parameter.

To enable block change tracking, execute the following ALTER DATABASE statement:

```
ALTER DATABASE ENABLE BLOCK CHANGE TRACKING;
```

You can also create the change tracking file in a specific location:

```
ALTER DATABASE ENABLE BLOCK CHANGE TRACKING
USING FILE '/ocpdir/rman_change_track.f' REUSE;
```

You can disable block change tracking by executing the following command:

```
ALTER DATABASE DISABLE BLOCK CHANGE TRACKING;
```

The V$BLOCK_CHANGE_TRACKING view can be used to determine whether change tracking is enabled, and the file name of the block change tracking file.

```
SELECT status, filename
FROM   v$block_change_tracking;

STATUS   FILENAME
-------- ---------------------------------------------------
ENABLED  /u01/ocp/RDBMS/changetracking/e1_cs_2e61nr6j_.chg
```

Report on backups using LIST, REPORT commands

A repository of RMAN metadata is always stored in the control file of each database on which it performs backup operations. In addition, a recovery catalog can be used to store metadata. When utilized, RMAN can store metadata for multiple target databases in a set of tables in a separate recovery catalog database. The LIST and REPORT commands provide a number of reports to aid in determining backup actions that have been (or should be) performed..

RMAN LIST Command

The LIST command uses the information in the RMAN repository to provide lists of backups and other objects relating to backup and recovery.

- **LIST BACKUP** -- Allows you to list all backup sets, copies, and proxy copies of a database, tablespace, datafile, archived redo log, control file, or server parameter file.
- **LIST COPY** -- Allows you to list datafile copies and archived redo log files. By default, LIST COPY displays copies of all database files and archived redo logs.
- **LIST ARCHIVELOG** -- Allows you to list archive redo log files. You can list all archive log redo log files or you specify individual archive log files through SCN, time, or sequence number ranges.
- **LIST INCARNATION** -- Allows you to list all incarnations of a database. A new database incarnation is created when you open with the RESETLOGS option.
- **LIST DB_UNIQUE_NAME** -- In a Data Guard environment, each database is distinguished by its DB_UNIQUE_NAME initialization parameter setting. You can list all databases that have the same DBID.
- **LIST ... FOR DB_UNIQUE_NAME** -- Allows you to list all backups and copies for a specified database in a Data Guard environment or for all databases in the environment.
- **LIST RESTORE POINT** -- Allows you to list restore points known to the RMAN repository.
- **LIST SCRIPT NAMES** -- Allows you to list the names of recovery catalog scripts created with the CREATE SCRIPT or REPLACE SCRIPT command.
- **LIST FAILURE** -- A failure is a persistent data corruption mapped to a repair option.

List has a number of options that enable you to control how output is displayed. Some of the most common LIST options are:

- **LIST EXPIRED** -- Lists backups or copies that are recorded in the RMAN repository but that were not present at the expected location on disk or tape during the most recent crosscheck.
- **LIST ... BY FILE** -- Lists backups of each datafile, archived redo log file, control file, and server parameter file. Each row describes a backup of a file.
- **LIST ... SUMMARY** -- Provides a one-line summary of each backup.

RMAN REPORT Command

The RMAN REPORT command performs an analysis of the available backups for your database. The results of this can be used to determine actions that should be taken, such as backing up specific files or removing obsolete backups to free up disk space. Some of the common uses of the REPORT command are:

- **REPORT NEED BACKUP** -- Reports which database files need to be backed up to meet a configured or specified retention policy.
- **REPORT UNRECOVERABLE** -- Reports which database files require backup because they have been affected by some NOLOGGING operation such as a direct-path INSERT.
- **REPORT OBSOLETE** -- Returns full backups, datafile copies, and archived redo logs recorded in the RMAN repository that can be deleted because they are no longer required.
- **REPORT SCHEMA** -- Returns the names of all datafiles and tablespaces for the target database at the specified point in time.

Manage backups using CROSSCHECK, DELETE commands

The CROSSCHECK command is used to ensure that the information regarding backups in the recovery catalog or control file is synchronized with corresponding data on disk or in the media management catalog. The CROSSCHECK command will only operate on files that are recorded in the recovery catalog or the control file. If archived logs are deleted from the physical disk using an operating system command, the RMAN repository will still indicate that the logs exist. The CROSSCHECK command will update outdated RMAN repository information about backups whose repository records do not match their physical status. When the backup is on disk, CROSSCHECK will determine whether the header of the file is valid. For backups that are on tape, the command only checks that the backup exists. The possible status values for backups are AVAILABLE, UNAVAILABLE, and EXPIRED.

The status of backups can be determined using the RMAN LIST command, or by querying V$BACKUP_FILES. If a recovery catalog exists, the status can be found in catalog views such as RC_DATAFILE_COPY and RC_ARCHIVED_LOG. For all backups in the RMAN repository, they will be marked as EXPIRED if the backup is no longer available. For backups that are marked as EXPIRED but are now available, RMAN will change the status to AVAILABLE.

Executing CROSSCHECK command does not delete operating system files. It also does not remove the RMAN repository records of backups that are not available. The only action taken is to update the repository records with the current status of the backups.

The DELETE EXPIRED command can be used to remove records of expired backups from the RMAN repository. If the expired files still exist, then the DELETE EXPIRED command will terminate with an error. The following example will delete expired repository records:

1. Issue a CROSSCHECK command.

   ```
   CROSSCHECK BACKUP;
   ```

2. Delete the expired backups.

   ```
   DELETE EXPIRED BACKUP;
   ```

Configuring RMAN Backup Options and Creating Backup of Non-Database Files

Use techniques to improve backups

Create compressed backups

For any use of the BACKUP command that creates backup sets, you can enable binary compression of backup sets by adding the AS COMPRESSED BACKUPSET option to the BACKUP command. RMAN will compress the backup set contents before writing to disk. Information regarding the binary compression level used is automatically recorded in the backup set. When recovering, there is no need to explicitly mention the type of compression used or how to decompress. Note that binary compression imposes a performance overhead during backup and restore operations. It consumes CPU resources, so compressed backups should not be scheduled when CPU usage is high.

Specifying the COMPRESSED option in the BACKUP TYPE TO ... BACKUPSET clause configures RMAN to use compressed backup sets by default for a given device type. Omitting the COMPRESSED keyword disables compression. The preconfigured backup type for disk is an uncompressed backup set (the equivalent of the following CONFIGURE command):

```
CONFIGURE DEVICE TYPE DISK BACKUP TYPE TO BACKUPSET;
```

To enable compression on backup sets by default, you can add the COMPRESSED keyword to the above command:

```
CONFIGURE DEVICE TYPE DISK BACKUP TYPE TO COMPRESSED BACKUPSET;
```

If the CONFIGURE command has been used to set the default backup type to compressed backup set, backups will use compression by default. It is also possible to enable compression explicitly for a single backup. An example of a command to make a compressed backup is:

```
BACKUP
AS COMPRESSED BACKUPSET
DATABASE PLUS ARCHIVELOG;
```

Create multi-section backups of very large files

Multisection backups enable RMAN channels to back up a single large file in parallel. The work is divided among multiple channels, with each channel backing up one file section in a file. This can improve the performance of backups of large datafiles. Multisection backups are enabled by specifying the SECTION SIZE parameter on the BACKUP command. Each file section is a contiguous range of blocks in a file. The SECTION SIZE parameter cannot be used in conjunction with MAXPIECESIZE. If the value of SECTION SIZE is larger than the file size, then RMAN will not use multisection backup for the file. If the section size would result in more than 256 file sections, then RMAN will increase the section size so that the result is exactly 256 sections. In the following example, the TOOLS tablespace contains a single datafile of 1 GB. The environment has two tape drives with channels allocated and the parallelism for SBT is set to two. The following command will break the tablespace datafile into two file 500MB file sections:

```
BACKUP
  SECTION SIZE 500M
  TABLESPACE tools;
```

Create proxy copies

When performing a proxy copy, RMAN turns over control of the data transfer to a media manager that supports this feature. Proxy copy cannot be used with channels of type DISK. The feature can only be used with media managers that support it. By giving the media manager more control over the data movement, CPU resources on the target node are reduced.

For each file that being backed up using the BACKUP PROXY command, RMAN will query the media manager to determine whether it can perform a proxy copy. If the media manager is unable to proxy copy the file, RMAN will back up the file as if the PROXY option had not been used. If the PROXY ONLY option is used, RMAN will fail if a proxy copy cannot be performed. Control files are never backed up with proxy copy. Backups with the PROXY option that include control files will ignore the option when backing up the control file.

Create duplexed backup sets

RMAN has the ability to create up to four duplexed copies when creating a backup set. Duplexing is not possible when making image copies. Duplexing is enabled using the COPIES parameter in the CONFIGURE, SET, or BACKUP commands. When duplexing, RMAN produces a single backup set with a unique key, and generates the requested number of identical copies of each backup piece in the set. It is possible to duplex backups to either disk or tape, but not to tape and disk simultaneously. The FORMAT parameter of the BACKUP command sets the destinations for the backup sets. The number of copies should never exceed the number of available tape devices when backup up to tape. Duplexing backup sets to the fast recovery area is not possible. The following command creates two backup set copies of data file 3:

```
BACKUP DEVICE TYPE DISK COPIES 2 DATAFILE 3
  FORMAT '/u01/%U','/u02/%U';
```

It is also possible to use CONFIGURE BACKUP COPIES to enable duplexing by default. The default setting will apply to all backup sets except control file autobackups and backupsets that are backed up using the BACKUP BACKUPSET command. By default, CONFIGURE ... BACKUP COPIES is set to 1 for disk and tape. The following example sets duplexing for datafiles and archivelog files on disk to two.

```
CONFIGURE CHANNEL DEVICE TYPE DISK FORMAT '/u01/%U', '/u02/%U';
CONFIGURE DATAFILE BACKUP COPIES FOR DEVICE TYPE DISK TO 2;
CONFIGURE ARCHIVELOG BACKUP COPIES FOR DEVICE TYPE DISK TO 2;
```

Given the above configuration, the following command backs up the database and archived logs to disk, making two copies of each data file and archived log, placing one copy of the backup sets produced in the /u01 directory and the other in the /u02 directory:

```
BACKUP DEVICE TYPE DISK AS BACKUPSET DATABASE PLUS ARCHIVELOG;
```

Create backups of backup sets

You can use RMAN to make copies of existing previously created backup sets with the BACKUP BACKUPSET command. This will back up backup sets that were created on disk and can be used to spread backups among multiple media. If RMAN determines that a backup set is corrupted or missing, it will search for other copies of the same backup set. The following example backs up existing backup sets to tape to ensure that all your backups exist on both media types.

```
BACKUP DEVICE TYPE DISK AS BACKUPSET
  DATABASE PLUS ARCHIVELOG;
BACKUP
  DEVICE TYPE sbt
  BACKUPSET ALL;
```

The BACKUP BACKUPSET can also be used to manage backup space allocation. The following backs up backup sets that were created more than 14 days ago from disk to tape, and then deletes the backup sets from disk. If a backup was duplexed to multiple locations on disk, RMAN will delete all copies of the pieces in the backup set.

```
BACKUP
  DEVICE TYPE SBT
  BACKUPSET COMPLETED BEFORE 'SYSDATE-14'
  DELETE INPUT;
```

Create archival backups

The RMAN KEEP option specifies that a backup be created as an archival backup. An archival backup is a self-contained backup that is exempt from the configured retention policy. Archival backups contain all of the files necessary to restore the backup and recover it to a consistent state. If the database is open at the time an archival backup is created, RMAN automatically generates and backs up the redo logs needed to make the backup consistent. When available, RMAN will use archival backups for disaster recovery restore operations. However, their intended purpose is to produce a snapshot of the database that can be restored on another system for testing or historical usage.

KEEP

When computing the retention policy RMAN does not consider backup pieces with the KEEP option. The KEEP option cannot be used to override the retention policy for files stored in the fast recovery area. When KEEP is specified, RMAN backs up datafiles, archived redo logs, the control file, and the server parameter file. A recovery catalog is required when KEEP FOREVER is specified because the backup records will eventually age out of the control file.

UNTIL TIME 'date_string'

This clause specifies an end date for retaining the RMAN backup or copy. After this date the backup is obsolete, regardless of the backup retention policy settings. It's possible to provide a specific date/time by using the current NLS_DATE_FORMAT, or a SQL date expression such as 'SYSDATE+90'. If a KEEP TIME is provided with a date only, then the backup becomes obsolete one second after midnight on that date.

RESTORE POINT restore_point_name

Creates a restore point matching the SCN to which RMAN must recover the backup to a consistent state. The name provided must not already exist. RMAN captures the SCN immediately after the datafile backups complete. The restore point acts as a label for the SCN to which this archival backup can be restored.

NOKEEP

This option indicates that any KEEP attributes no longer apply to the backup. After specifying NOKEEP, the backup is subject to the configured backup retention

Perform backup of non-database files

Back up a control file to trace

It is possible to back up the control file to a text file that contains a CREATE CONTROLFILE statement. This trace file can then be edited to generate a script to create a new control file based on the one that was current when the trace was created. The trace file will be created in a subdirectory determined by the DIAGNOSTIC_DEST initialization parameter. The database alert log will also contain the name and location of the newly created trace file. The steps to back up the control file to a trace file are:

1. Mount or open the database.
2. Execute the following SQL statement:

```
ALTER DATABASE BACKUP CONTROLFILE TO TRACE;
```

Back up archived redo log files

The BACKUP ARCHIVELOG command is used to back up archived logs. If backup optimization has been enabled, RMAN will skip backups of archived logs that have already been backed up to the specified device. The steps to back up archived redo log files are:

1. Start RMAN and connect to a target database and a recovery catalog (if used).
2. Ensure that the target database is mounted or open.
3. Execute the BACKUP ARCHIVELOG or BACKUP ... PLUS ARCHIVELOG command.
   The following example backs up the database and all archived redo logs:

   ```
   BACKUP DATABASE PLUS ARCHIVELOG;
   ```

   The following example backs up one copy of each log sequence number for all archived redo logs:

   ```
   BACKUP ARCHIVELOG ALL;
   ```

Back up ASM diskgroup metadata

The ASM command-line utility (ASMCMD) allows ASM disk identification, disk bad block repair, and backup and restore operations of your ASM environment for faster recovery, among other capabilities. ASMCMD allows ASM diskgroup data to be backed up using the md_backup command. The MD_BACKUP command creates a file containing the metadata for one or more disk groups. The backup file can be used to restore disk groups rapidly in the event of a catastrophic failure of the ASM instance. By default all the mounted disk groups are included in the backup file which is saved in the current working directory. If the name of the backup file is not specified, ASM names the file AMBR_BACKUP_INTERMEDIATE_FILE.

The syntax of the md_backup command is:

```
md_backup [-b location_of_backup] [-g dgname [-g dgname …]]
```

Where:

-b Specifies the location in which you want to store the backup file

-g Specifies the disk group name to be backed up. Multiple diskgroups can be specified by repeating the –g option

Using RMAN-Encrypted Backups

Create RMAN-encrypted backups

Use transparent-mode encryption

RMAN allows backup sets to be created using encryption. If files of the backup sets are obtained by unauthorized users, they cannot be read or used to restore a database. Encryption can be transparent, which is based on an encryption key stored in Oracle Wallet. Alternately it can be password-based, which makes use of a user-supplied password. Dual-mode encryption combines both wallet and password-based encryption. The following commands are used to activate and modify the default encryption behavior of RMAN:

- **CONFIGURE ENCRYPTION** -- This command can be used to configure RMAN to perform transparent encryption of backup sets by default. It is not possible to persistently configure dual mode or password mode encryption.
- **SET ENCRYPTION** -- This command is used to configure dual mode or password mode encryption at the RMAN session level.

The default algorithm used for encrypting backups is AES 128-bit. However, it is possible to use any of the values listed in V$RMAN_ENCRYPTION_ALGORITHMS. The CONFIGURE command can be used to persistently configure the default algorithm to another value:

1. Start RMAN and connect to a target database and a recovery catalog (if used).
2. Ensure that the target database is mounted or open.
3. Execute the CONFIGURE ENCRYPTION ALGORITHM command. The following example set RMAN to use AES 256-bit encryption:

```
CONFIGURE ENCRYPTION ALGORITHM TO 'AES256';
```

If the CONFIGURE command is used to enable transparent encryption, no additional action is required to make encrypted backups. RMAN backups will be encrypted by default. To make transparent-mode encrypted backups, the default encryption mode must have been set:

```
CONFIGURE ENCRYPTION FOR DATABASE ON;
```

Once the mode has been set, backups will require no additional syntax to be encrypted:

1. Start RMAN and connect to a target database and recovery catalog (if used).
2. Back up the database.

```
BACKUP DATABASE PLUS ARCHIVELOG;
```

Use password-mode encryption

It is not possible to configure password-mode encryption to occur by default. Creating a password-encrypted backup set requires the session to be specifically configured. To make password-mode encrypted backups:

1. Start RMAN and connect to a target database and recovery catalog (if used).
2. Execute the SET ENCRYPTION ON IDENTIFIED BY password ONLY command.

```
SET ENCRYPTION ON IDENTIFIED BY password ONLY FOR ALL
TABLESPACES;
```

3. Back up the database.

```
BACKUP DATABASE PLUS ARCHIVELOG;
```

Use dual-mode encryption

The value of dual-mode encrypted backups is that it is possible to restore them either transparently or by specifying the encryption password. This might be used when backups are normally restored on-site using the Oracle keystore, but might have a requirement to be restored at another site that does not have access to the Oracle keystore. To create a dual-mode encrypted backup set:

1. Start RMAN and connect to a target database and recovery catalog (if used).
2. Execute the SET ENCRYPTION ON IDENTIFIED BY password command.

   ```
   SET ENCRYPTION ON IDENTIFIED BY password FOR ALL TABLESPACES;
   ```

3. Back up the database.

Restore encrypted backups

A single restore operation can process backups encrypted in different modes. When restoring each backup piece, RMAN will determine whether or not it is encrypted. If the Oracle keystore is open and available, backups created using transparent encryption need no intervention. If RMAN detects a backup piece that has used password encryption, it searches for a matching key in the list of passwords provided in the SET DECRYPTION command. If it locates a usable key, the restore operation will proceed. If no usable key is found in the SET DECRYPTION command, RMAN searches for a key in the Oracle keystore. If it locates a usable key, then the restore operation proceeds. If no key is found in the keystore, RMAN signals an error that the backup piece cannot be decrypted.

Diagnosing Failures

Describe the Automatic Diagnostic Workflow

Use the Automatic Diagnostic Repository

The Automatic Diagnostic Repository (ADR) is a directory structure for diagnostic files such as traces, dumps, the alert log, health monitor reports, and more. The directory structure supports multiple instances and multiple Oracle products. Each instance of each product will store diagnostic data underneath its own home directory within the ADR. It provides a unified directory structure along with consistent diagnostic data formats across products and instances. This plus a unified set of tools enables diagnostic data to be correlated and analyzed across multiple Oracle products.

Because all diagnostic data, including the alert log, is stored in the ADR, the initialization parameters BACKGROUND_DUMP_DEST and USER_DUMP_DEST have been deprecated. They have been replaced by the initialization parameter DIAGNOSTIC_DEST. The DIAGNOSTIC_DEST parameter identifies the directory which serves as the ADR Base location.

The V$DIAG_INFO view lists all the important ADR locations for the current Oracle database instance. It also provides the number of active problems and incidents and the tracefiles for the current instance.

- **ADR Base** -- Path of ADR base
- **ADR Home** -- Path of ADR home for the current database instance
- **Diag Trace** -- Location of background process trace files, server process trace files, SQL trace files, and the text-formatted version of the alert log
- **Diag Alert** -- Location of the XML-formatted version of the alert log
- **Default Trace** -- File Path to the trace file for the current session
- **Diag Incident** -- File path for incident packages
- **Diag Cdump** -- Equivalent to cdump. Location for core dump files.
- **Health Monitor** -- Location for health monitor output.

```
SELECT name, value
FROM   v$diag_info;

NAME VALUE
-------------------- ---------------------------------------------------
----
Diag Enabled          TRUE
ADR Base              /u01/oracle
ADR Home              /u01/oracle/diag/rdbms/orclbi/orclbi
Diag Trace            /u01/oracle/diag/rdbms/orclbi/orclbi/trace
Diag Alert            /u01/oracle/diag/rdbms/orclbi/orclbi/alert
Diag Incident         /u01/oracle/diag/rdbms/orclbi/orclbi/incident
Diag Cdump            /u01/oracle/diag/rdbms/orclbi/orclbi/cdump
Health Monitor        /u01/oracle/diag/rdbms/orclbi/orclbi/hm
Default Trace File
/u01/oracle/diag/rdbms/orclbi/orclbi/trace/orcl_ora_22459.trc
Active Problem Count  8
Active Incident Count 20
```

Use ADRCI

The Automatic Diagnostic Repository Command Interpreter (ADRCI) is a command-line utility that is part of the fault diagnosability infrastructure. ADRCI's primary functions include:

- Viewing diagnostic data in the Automatic Diagnostic Repository.
- Viewing Health Monitor reports.
- Packaging incident and problem information for Oracle Support.

Diagnostic data viewable from within ADRCI includes incident and problem descriptions, trace files, dumps, health monitor reports, alert log entries, and more. ADRCI can be used in interactive mode or within scripts. ADRCI can also execute scripts of ADRCI commands just as SQL*Plus can execute scripts of SQL and PL/SQL commands. There is no login to ADRCI -- it is secured by OS-level file permissions only.

An ADR home is the root directory for all diagnostic data for a particular instance of a given Oracle product or component. All ADR homes share the same hierarchical directory structure that starts at the ADR_BASE directory. Some ADRCI commands can work with multiple ADR homes simultaneously while others require that a single ADR home be set within ADRCI before issuing the command. The current ADRCI homepath determines the ADR homes that are searched for diagnostic data when an ADRCI command is issued. It does so by pointing to a specific directory within the ADR base hierarchy. When pointed to a single ADR home directory, that ADR home is the only current ADR home. If the homepath points to a higher directory, all ADR homes that are below the directory that is pointed to become current. The ADR homepath is null by default when ADRCI starts, which means that all the ADR homes beneath the ADR_BASE are current. The SHOW HOME and SHOW HOMEPATH commands display the current ADR homes. The SET HOMEPATH command sets the homepath to a specific directory.

The alert log is written as both an XML-formatted file and as a plain text file. You can view either format with any text editor. Alternately, you can use ADRCI to view the XML-formatted alert log with the XML tags stripped. By default, ADRCI displays the alert log in your default editor. You can use the SET EDITOR command to change the editor used by ADRCI.

You can use ADRCI to view the names of trace files that are currently in the ADR. You can view the names of all trace files, or a filtered subset of names. ADRCI has commands to obtain a list of trace files whose file name matches a search string, exist in a particular directory, pertain to a particular incident, or a combination of these. The SHOW TRACEFILE command displays a list of the files in the trace directory and in all incident directories under the current ADR home.

The ADRCI SHOW INCIDENT command can be used to display information about open incidents. For each incident, the incident ID, problem key, and incident creation time are shown. If the ADRCI homepath includes multiple current ADR homes, the report displays incidents from all of them.

```
SHOW INCIDENT
ADR Home =
/u03/app/oracle/product/11.1.0/db_2/log/diag/rdbms/orcl12c/orcl12c:
*************************************************************************
INCIDENT_ID       PROBLEM_KEY              CREATE_TIME
--------------- ----------------- ---------------------------------
4218            ORA 603               2011-03-18 21:35:49.322161 -07:00
4219            ORA 600 [4134]        2011-03-20 21:35:47.862114 -07:00
4224            ORA 600 [4138]        2011-04-01 21:35:25.012579 -07:00
3 rows fetched
```

The following are variations on the SHOW INCIDENT command:

```
SHOW INCIDENT -MODE BRIEF
SHOW INCIDENT -MODE DETAIL
SHOW INCIDENT -MODE DETAIL -P "INCIDENT_ID=1681"
```

Find and interpret message output and error stacks

RMAN generates several different types of output that can be useful in diagnosing problems. These include:

- **RMAN messages** -- RMAN stores completed job information in V$RMAN_STATUS and RC_RMAN_STATUS. Information for current jobs is stored in V$RMAN_OUTPUT. When RMAN is run from the command line, it is also possible to direct output to standard output, a log file, or a file created by redirecting RMAN output.
- **alert_SID.log** -- The Oracle server will write output to the alert log, in the alert subdirectory of the Automatic Diagnostic Repository (ADR) home. It contains a chronological log of errors, initialization parameter settings, and administration operations.
- **Oracle trace file** -- The Oracle server will create trace files in the trace subdirectory of the ADR home. Trace files contain detailed output generated by Oracle Database processes. A trace file is created when an ORA-600 or ORA-3113 error message occurs, whenever RMAN cannot allocate a channel, and when the database fails to load the media management library.

- **sbtio.log** -- Third-party media management software can create this file in the trace subdirectory of the ADR home. It contains vendor-specific information written by the media management software.

RMAN error stacks are covered in a later chapter devoted specifically to them. Why Oracle certification has two chapters for this exam that reference RMAN error stacks is one of the world's great mysteries.

Use the Data Recovery Advisor

Oracle's Data Recovery Advisor is a data corruption repair function integrated with Support Workbench, database health checks and RMAN. It can display data corruption problems, assess their extent and impact, recommend repair options, and automate the repair process. In the context of Data Recovery Advisor, a health check is a diagnostic procedure run by the Health Monitor to assess the state of the database or its components. Health checks are invoked reactively when an error occurs and can also be invoked manually. Data Recovery Advisor can diagnose failures such as the following:

- Components such as data files and control files that are not accessible by the database.
- Physical corruptions such as block checksum failures and invalid block header field values.
- Inconsistencies such as a data file that is older than other database files.
- I/O failures such as hardware errors, operating system driver failures, and exceeding operating system resource limits.

In some cases, the Data Recovery Advisor may be able to detect or handle logical corruptions. As a general rule, detecting and repairing logical corruptions will require assistance from Oracle Support Services.

Failures

A failure is a persistent data corruption detected by a health check. They are usually detected reactively when a database operation encounters corrupted data and generates an error. This will automatically invoke a health check in the database. The check will search the database for failures related to the error and record any findings in the Automatic Diagnostic Repository. Data Recovery Advisor can generate repair advice and repair failures only after failures have been detected by the database and stored in the ADR. Data Recovery Advisor can report on and repair failures such as inaccessible files, physical and logical block corruptions, and I/O failures. All failures are assigned a priority: CRITICAL, HIGH, or LOW, and a status of OPEN or CLOSED.

- **CRITICAL** priority failures require immediate attention because they make the whole database unavailable. Typically, critical failures bring down the instance and are diagnosed during the subsequent startup.
- **HIGH** priority failures make a database partially unavailable or unrecoverable, and usually have to be repaired in a reasonably short time.
- **LOW** priority indicates that failures can be ignored until more important failures are fixed.

DRA Repairs

Data Recovery Advisor allows you to view repair options. Repairs might involve the use of block media recovery, datafile media recovery, or Oracle Flashback Database. In general, Data Recovery Advisor presents both automated and manual repair options. If appropriate, you can choose an automated repair option in order to perform a repair. In an automated repair, Data Recovery Advisor performs the repair, verifies the repair success, and closes the relevant failures.

The recommended workflow for repairing data failures from RMAN is to run the following commands in sequence during an RMAN session: LIST FAILURE to display failures, ADVISE FAILURE to display repair options, and REPAIR FAILURE to fix the failures.

LIST FAILURE

The LIST FAILURE command displays failures against which you can run the ADVISE FAILURE and REPAIR FAILURE commands.

```
RMAN> LIST FAILURE;
List of Database Failures
=========================
Failure ID Priority Status  Time Detected Summary
---------- -------- ------ -------------- ----------------------
274        HIGH     OPEN    21-FEB-14     One or more non-system
                                          datafiles are missing
329        HIGH     OPEN    21-FEB-14     Datafile 1:
                                          '/u01/oradata/prod/
                                           system01.dbf'
                                          contains one or more
                                          corrupt blocks
```

ADVISE FAILURE

Use the ADVISE FAILURE command to display repair options for the specified failures. This command prints a summary of the failures identified by the Data Recovery Advisor and implicitly closes all open failures that are already fixed. The ADVISE FAILURE command indicates the repair strategy that Data Recovery Advisor considers optimal for a given set of failures. Data Recovery Advisor verifies repair feasibility before proposing a repair strategy. For example, it will check that all backups and archived redo log files needed for media recovery are available. It can generate both manual and automated repair options.

The ADVISE command maps a set of failures to the set of repair steps that Data Recovery Advisor considers to be optimal. When possible, Data Recovery Advisor consolidates multiple repair steps into a single repair. For example, if the database has corrupted datafile, missing control file, and lost current redo log group, then Data Recovery Advisor would recommend a single, consolidated repair plan to restore the database and perform point-in-time recovery.

```
RMAN> ADVISE FAILURE;
List of Database Failures
=========================
Failure ID Priority Status  Time Detected Summary
---------- -------- ------ -------------- ----------------------
274        HIGH     OPEN   21-FEB-14      One or more non-system
                                          datafiles are missing
329        HIGH     OPEN   21-FEB-14      Datafile 1:
                                          '/u01/oradata/prod/
                                           system01.dbf'
                                          contains one or more
                                          corrupt blocks

analyzing automatic repair options; this may take some time
using channel ORA_DISK_1
analyzing automatic repair options complete

Mandatory Manual Actions
========================
no manual actions available

Optional Manual Actions
=======================
1. If file /u01/oradata/prod/data01.dbf was unintentionally renamed
or moved, restore it

Automated Repair Options
========================
Option Repair Description
--- ----------
Restore and recover datafile 31; Perform block
    media recovery of block 43481 in file 1

Strategy: The repair includes complete media recovery with no data
loss
Repair script:
/u01/oracle/log/diag/rdbms/prod/prod/hm/reco_740113269.hm
```

CHANGE FAILURE

The CHANGE FAILURE command allows you to change the failure priority from HIGH to LOW or the reverse, or to close it. You cannot change to or from CRITICAL priority.

```
RMAN> CHANGE FAILURE 3 PRIORITY LOW;
```

REPAIR FAILURE

The REPAIR FAILURE command is used to repair database failures identified by the Data Recovery Advisor. The target database instance must be started, it must be a single-instance database and cannot be a physical standby database. It is important that at most one RMAN session is running the REPAIR FAILURE command. The only exception is REPAIR FAILURE ... PREVIEW, which is permitted in concurrent RMAN sessions. To perform an automated repair, the Data Recovery Advisor may require specific backups and archived redo logs. If the files are not available, then the recovery will not be possible. Data Recovery Advisor consolidates repairs whenever possible so that a single repair can fix multiple failures. If one has not yet been issued in the current RMAN session, REPAIR FAILURE performs an implicit ADVISE FAILURE. RMAN always verifies that failures are still relevant and automatically closes failures that have already been repaired. After executing a repair, RMAN reevaluates all open failures on the chance that some of them may also have been fixed.

Handle block corruption

Detect block corruption using RMAN

The VALIDATE command of RMAN can be used to manually check for physical and logical corruptions in database files. The command performs the same types of checks as BACKUP VALIDATE, but VALIDATE has the ability to check a larger selection of objects. When validating files, RMAN will check every block of the input file. If a previously unmarked corrupt block is discovered, RMAN will update the V$DATABASE_BLOCK_CORRUPTION view with rows describing the corruptions. Some of the possible targets for the VALIDATE command include:

- **VALIDATE BACKUPSET** -- This command checks every block in a backup set to ensure that the backup can be restored. If RMAN finds block corruption, then it issues an error and terminates the validation.
- **VALIDATE DATABASE** -- This command will validate all data files, control files and the server parameter file if one is in use.
- **VALIDATE DATAFILE 1** -- This command will validate the specified datafile.
- **VALIDATE DATAFILE 1 BLOCK 10** -- This command will validate a single block within the specified datafile.

If a large data file must be validated, it is possible for RMAN to perform the work in parallel by dividing the file into sections and processing each file section simultaneously. Multiple channels must be allocated and the SECTION SIZE parameter specified in the VALIDATE command. The following example performs parallel validation of a data file:

1. Start RMAN and connect to a target database. The target database must be mounted or open.
2. Run VALIDATE with the SECTION SIZE parameter.

```
RUN
{
ALLOCATE CHANNEL c1 DEVICE TYPE DISK;
ALLOCATE CHANNEL c2 DEVICE TYPE DISK;
VALIDATE DATAFILE 1 SECTION SIZE 600M;
}
```

The BACKUP VALIDATE command can also be used to detect block corruption. It can be used to perform the following functions:

- Check data files for physical and logical block corruption
- Confirm that all database files exist and are in the correct locations

During the BACKUP VALIDATE operation, RMAN reads the files to be backed up in their entirety. The operation does not produce any backup sets or image copies. It is not possible to use the BACKUPSET, MAXCORRUPT, or PROXY parameters with the BACKUP VALIDATE command. The following example validate that all database files and archived logs contain no physical corruptions and can be backed up:

1. Start RMAN and connect to a target database and recovery catalog (if used).
2. Run the BACKUP VALIDATE command.

```
BACKUP VALIDATE
DATABASE
ARCHIVELOG ALL;
```

In order to check for logical corruptions in addition to physical corruptions, the CHECK LOGICAL option must be added to the preceding command:

```
BACKUP VALIDATE
CHECK LOGICAL
DATABASE
ARCHIVELOG ALL;
```

The RESTORE ... VALIDATE command is used to test whether RMAN can restore a specific file or set of files from a backup. The database must be mounted or open for this command, but there is no need to take data files offline. Validating backups of the data files only reads the backups and does not affect the production data files. The following example shows how to validate backups with the RESTORE command:

1. Run the RESTORE command with the VALIDATE option.

```
RESTORE DATABASE VALIDATE;
RESTORE ARCHIVELOG ALL VALIDATE;
```

If no error stack is generated, then RMAN can use these backups successfully during a real restore and recovery.

It is possible to validate a CDB in much the same fashion as a non-CDB. The primary difference is that you must connect to the root as a common user with the common SYSBACKUP or SYSDBA privilege.

The following command, when connected to the root, validates the whole CDB:

```
VALIDATE DATABASE;
```

The following command validates the root:

```
VALIDATE DATABASE ROOT;
```

The following command, when connected to the root, validates the PDBs ocp_pdb and dev_pdb.

```
VALIDATE PLUGGABLE DATABASE ocp_pdb, dev_pdb;
```

The following command, when connected to a PDB, validates only the current PDB.

```
VALIDATE DATABASE;
```

The following command, when connected to a PDB, validates the restore of the database.

```
RESTORE DATABASE VALIDATE;
```

Perform block recovery using RMAN

Block media recovery allows you to recover individual corrupt data blocks within a data file. It is faster than data file media recovery because only blocks that need recovery are restored and recovered. Also, unlike data file media recovery, the affected data files remain online during the recovery process. Prior to the block media recovery capability, a single corrupt block in a datafile required taking the data file offline and restoring from backup.

When the database encounters a corrupt block, it marks the block as media corrupt and then writes it to disk. After being marked corrupt, no subsequent read of the block will be successful until the block is recovered. If block corruption has been detected, block media recovery can be performed manually using the RECOVER ... BLOCK command. By default, RMAN first searches for good blocks in the real-time query physical standby database (if one exists), then flashback logs and then blocks in full or level 0 incremental backups.

All known corrupted block in the database can be located by querying the V$DATABASE_BLOCK_CORRUPTION view. It contains blocks marked corrupt by database components such as RMAN, ANALYZE, dbv, and SQL queries. The following types of corruption result in the addition of rows to this view:

- **Physical corruption** -- Physical corruption, also known as media corruption, means that the database does not recognize the block: the checksum is invalid, the block contains all zeros, or the block header is corrupt. Physical corruption checking is enabled by default. Checksum checking can be disabled by specifying the NOCHECKSUM option of the BACKUP command, but other physical consistency checks cannot be disabled.
- **Logical corruption** -- Logical corruption occurs when the block has a valid checksum, the header and footer match, and so on, but the contents are logically inconsistent. Logical corruption cannot always be corrected by block media recovery. It may be necessary to use alternate recovery methods, such as tablespace point-in-time recovery, or dropping and re-creating the affected objects. Logical corruption checking is disabled by default. It can be enabled by specifying the CHECK LOGICAL option of the BACKUP, RESTORE, RECOVER, and VALIDATE commands.

The following prerequisites apply to the RECOVER ... BLOCK command:

- The target database must run in ARCHIVELOG mode and be open or mounted with a current control file.
- If the target database is a standby database, then it must be in a consistent state, recovery cannot be in session, and the backup must be older than the corrupted file.
- The backups of the data files containing the corrupt blocks must be full or level 0 backups and not proxy copies.
- RMAN can use only archived redo logs for the recovery.
- Flashback Database must be enabled on the target database for RMAN to search the flashback logs for good copies of corrupt blocks.
- The target database must be associated with a real-time query physical standby database for RMAN to search a standby database for good copies of corrupt blocks.

Recovering Individual Blocks

To recover specific data blocks, you must obtain the data file numbers and block numbers of the corrupted blocks. When Oracle encounters a corrupted block, you may get an error in a trace file like the following:

```
ORA-01578: ORACLE data block corrupted (file # 4, block # 213)
ORA-01110: data file 4: '/oracle/oradata/trgt/users01.dbf'
```

To recover this block, perform the following steps:

1. Start RMAN and connect to the target database, which must be mounted or open.
2. Run the SHOW ALL command to confirm that the appropriate channels are preconfigured.
3. Run the RECOVER ... BLOCK command at the RMAN prompt, specifying the file and block numbers for the corrupted blocks.

```
RECOVER
DATAFILE 4 BLOCK 213;
```

Recovering All Blocks in V$DATABASE_BLOCK_CORRUPTION

Rather than recovering blocks individually, you can have RMAN automatically recover all blocks listed in the V$DATABASE_BLOCK_CORRUPTION view. The steps to do this are:

1. Start SQL*Plus and connect to the target database.
2. Query V$DATABASE_BLOCK_CORRUPTION to determine whether corrupt blocks exist.

```
SELECT * FROM V$DATABASE_BLOCK_CORRUPTION;
```

3. Start RMAN and connect to the target database.
4. Recover all blocks marked corrupt in V$DATABASE_BLOCK_CORRUPTION.

```
RMAN> RECOVER CORRUPTION LIST;
```

Once recovered, the blocks will automatically be removed from the view.

Performing Restore and Recovery Operations

Describe and tune instance recovery

Instance and crash recovery is the automatic application of redo log records to data blocks after a crash or system failure. Any time an instance is shut down cleanly, changes that are in memory but have not been written to the data files are written to disk during the shutdown checkpoint. However, if a database is shutdown with the abort option, or a single instance database crashes or if all instances of an Oracle RAC configuration crash, then this checkpoint does not occur. In these cases, the Oracle Database will perform a crash recovery on the next startup. There are two steps to instance and crash recovery: cache recovery followed by transaction recovery. Because the database can be opened once cache recovery completes, improving the performance of this step increases availability.

- **Cache Recovery** – In the cache recovery step (also known as rolling forward), the Database applies all committed and uncommitted changes in the redo log files to the affected data blocks. The amount of work required for cache recovery is proportional to the rate of change for the database and the time between checkpoints.
- **Transaction Recovery** – Once all changes from the redo log are applied to the data files, any changes that were not committed at the time of the crash must be rolled back. In the transaction recovery step, the database uses rollback information to back out the uncommitted changes.

Periodically, Oracle Database records the highest system change number (SCN) for which all data blocks less than or equal to that SCN are known to be written out to the data files. This is called a checkpoint. If there is an instance failure, only redo records with changes above the last checkpoint SCN must be applied during recovery. The duration of cache recovery processing is determined by two factors: the number of data blocks that have changes at SCNs higher than the SCN of the checkpoint, and the number of log blocks that need to be read to find those changes. A database that checkpoints frequently will write dirty buffers to the data files more often. This will reduce cache recovery time in the event of an instance failure because fewer redo blocks will have to be applied to the datafiles. However, frequent checkpointing in a high-update system can reduce database performance.

Oracle's Fast-Start Fault Recovery feature is intended to reduce cache recovery time and make it predictable. It does this by limiting the number of dirty buffers and the number of redo records generated between the most recent redo record and the last checkpoint. This feature uses the Fast-Start checkpointing architecture instead of conventional event-driven checkpointing. Instead of the bulk writes used by conventional checkpointing, fast-start checkpointing occurs incrementally. Each DBWn process periodically writes buffers to disk to advance the checkpoint position. This eliminates the I/O spikes that occur with conventional checkpointing. The FAST_START_MTTR_TARGET initialization parameter enables Fast-Start Fault Recovery and simplifies the configuration of recovery time from instance or system failure. The parameter sets a target for the expected mean time to recover (MTTR). The value of parameter is the time (in seconds) that it should take to start up the instance and perform cache recovery. Once set, the database manages incremental checkpoints in an attempt to meet that target.

Perform complete and incomplete recovery

Use RMAN RESTORE and RECOVER commands

The RESTORE and RECOVER commands are used for the restoration and recovery of physical database files. The RESTORE command retrieves files from backups as needed for a recovery operation. The RECOVER command performs media recovery. Media recovery is the application of changes from redo logs and incremental backups to a restored data file in order to bring the data file forward to a desired SCN or point in time

In order to use the RESTORE DATABASE and RECOVER DATABASE commands to recover the database, backups of all needed files must have been taken and be accessible. This example below assumes that it is possible restore all data files to their original locations. The following example uses the RESTORE AND RECOVER commands to recover the whole database:

1. Start RMAN and connect to the target database.
2. Optionally, list the current tablespaces and data files, as shown in the following command:

```
RMAN> REPORT SCHEMA;
```

3. Run the RESTORE DATABASE command with the PREVIEW option.

```
RMAN> RESTORE DATABASE PREVIEW SUMMARY;
```

4. Place the database in a mounted state.

```
RMAN> STARTUP FORCE MOUNT;
```

5. Restore the database.

```
RMAN> RESTORE DATABASE;
```

6. Recover the database, as shown in the following example:

```
RMAN> RECOVER DATABASE;
```

7. Open the database, as shown in the following example:

```
RMAN> ALTER DATABASE OPEN;
```

Restore ASM disk groups

The ASM command-line utility (ASMCMD) provides the ability to backup and restore the metadata for ASM disk groups. Earlier in this guide, the ASMCMD command **md_backup** was introduced. This command is used to create a backup of disk group metadata. The **md_restore** command is the complement to the **md_backup** command. It uses a previously created ASM metadata backup file to recreate diskgroups in an ASM instance.

The syntax of the md_restore command is:

```
md_restore -b backup_file
```

- **-b** -- Specifies the backup_file.
- **-I** -- Ignore errors. Normally, if md_restore encounters an error, it will stop.
- **-t** -- Specifies the type of disk group to be created:
- **full** -- Create disk group and restore metadata
- **nodg** -- Restore metadata only.
- **newdg** -- Create disk group with a different name and restore metadata; -o is required.
- **-f** -- Write SQL commands to <sql_script_file> instead of executing them.
- **-g** -- Select the disk groups to be restored. If left off, all disk groups will be restored.
- **-o** -- Rename disk group old_diskgroup_name to new_diskgroup_name.

Recover from media failures

A media failure occurs when there is a physical problem with a drive that stores one or more files used by the Oracle database. The physical problem causes a failure of a read from or write to a disk file that is required to run the database. The elements affected can be any of the files used by Oracle, including the data files, archived redo log files, or control file. Any time that a media failure is detected by Oracle, it takes the affected files offline. The appropriate recovery technique following a media failure depends on the files affected and the types of backup available.

The most common form of recovery following a media failure is data file media recovery. This involves restoring data file backups and applying archived redo logs or incremental backups to recover lost changes. When using data file media recovery, it is possible to either recover a whole database or a subset of the database. Data file media recovery is the most general-purpose form of recovery and can protect against both physical and logical failures. A number of the following chapters deal with specific subsets of data file media recovery.

Perform complete and incomplete or "point-in-time" recoveries using RMAN

Incomplete recovery of a database, also known as Database Point-In-Time recovery (DBPITR) restores a database to a time earlier than the one that is the target time. It then uses incremental backups and/or redo to roll the database forward until the target point is reached. It is possible to recover to a specific time, SCN, log sequence number, or restore point. Creating restore points at important times is recommended to make PITR easier if it is required. If it is possible to perform a Flashback Database operation to the desired point, then this is a considerably easier option than performing DBPITR through media recovery. In order to perform DBPITR, the following pre-requisites must be met:

- The database must be running in ARCHIVELOG mode.
- There must be backups of all data files from before the target SCN and archived logs for the period between the SCN of the backups and the target SCN.

When performing DBPITR, setting the target time using the SET UNTIL command at the beginning of the procedure reduces the potential for problems. Specifying the UNTIL clause on the RESTORE and RECOVER commands individually has the potential to restore backups that are not early enough to be used in the RECOVER operation. The DBPITR example below makes the following assumptions:

- The DBPITR is being performed within the current database incarnation.
- The control file is current.
- The database is using the current server parameter file.

1. Determine the time, SCN, restore point, or log sequence that ends recovery.
2. When using a target time expression instead of a target SCN, verify the time format environment variables before invoking RMAN.
3. Connect RMAN to the target database and, if applicable, the recovery catalog database. The database should be set to MOUNT status:

```
SHUTDOWN IMMEDIATE;
STARTUP MOUNT;
```

4. Perform the following operations within a RUN block:
    - Use SET UNTIL to specify the target time, SCN, or log sequence number, or SET TO when specifying a restore point.
    - If automatic channels are not configured, then manually allocate disk and tape channels as needed.
    - Restore and recover the database.

```
RUN
{
SET UNTIL SCN 123456;
RESTORE DATABASE;
RECOVER DATABASE;
}
```

Alternately, the SET line can use time expressions, restore points, or log sequence numbers:

```
SET UNTIL TIME '12-JAN-2014 12:00:00';
SET UNTIL SEQUENCE 4397;
SET TO RESTORE POINT fy2015_end;
```

5. If the operation completes with no errors, open the database read-only in SQL*Plus. Perform queries as needed to ensure that the database contains the desired information.

```
ALTER DATABASE OPEN READ ONLY;
```

6. If you are satisfied with the results, then open the database for read/write, abandoning all changes after the target SCN. The database must be shut down, remounted, and then opened with RESETLOGS:

```
SHUTDOWN IMMEDIATE;
STARTUP MOUNT;
ALTER DATABASE OPEN RESETLOGS;
```

Performing a complete recovery is less complex than an incomplete recovery. There is no requirement to pick a point to end the recovery at and there is no need to use the RESETLOGS command when opening the database after the recovery operation is complete.

1. Connect RMAN to the target database and, if applicable, the recovery catalog database. The database should be set to MOUNT status:

```
SHUTDOWN IMMEDIATE;
STARTUP MOUNT;
```

2. Perform the following operations within a RUN block:
   - If automatic channels are not configured, then manually allocate disk and tape channels as needed.
   - Restore and recover the database.

```
RUN
{
RESTORE DATABASE;
RECOVER DATABASE;
}
```

3. If the operation completes with no errors, open the database in SQL*Plus

```
ALTER DATABASE OPEN;
```

Recovering Files Using RMAN

Perform recovery for spfile, control file, redo log files

When the server parameter file of a database is lost, RMAN can restore the file to its default location or to a specified location. Losing the server parameter file does not cause the instance to immediately stop. However, the instance must be shut down and restarted after restoring the file. There are several considerations when restoring the server parameter file:

- If an instance is started with a given server parameter file, then the existing file cannot be overwritten.
- When the instance has been started with a client-side initialization parameter file, RMAN will restores the server parameter file to the default location unless the TO clause is used in the restore command.
- Restoring an SPFILE is simplified when a recovery catalog is used because it contains the DBID.

The steps to restore the server parameter file from autobackup are:

1. Start RMAN.
2. If the database instance is started, then connect to the target database. If the instance is not started and a recovery catalog is not being used, run the SET DBID command to set the DBID of the target database.
3. Shut down the database instance and restart it to NOMOUNT status.

```
STARTUP FORCE NOMOUNT;
```

4. Execute a RUN command to restore the server parameter file. The following example restores a server parameter file from an autobackup on tape:

```
RUN
{
ALLOCATE CHANNEL c1 DEVICE TYPE sbt PARMS ...;
SET UNTIL TIME 'SYSDATE-4';
SET CONTROLFILE AUTOBACKUP FORMAT
FOR DEVICE TYPE sbt TO '/u01/control_files/autobackup_%F';
SET DBID 348745982;
RESTORE SPFILE
TO '/tmp/spfileOCP.ora'
FROM AUTOBACKUP MAXDAYS 8;
}
```

5. Restart the database instance with the restored file.

If control file autobackups have been configured, the server parameter file will be backed up with the control file whenever an autobackup is taken. When restoring the server parameter file from a control file autobackup, the DBID for your database must be set before executing the RESTORE SPFILE FROM AUTOBACKUP command. If the autobackup is in a non-default format, the SET CONTROLFILE AUTOBACKUP FORMAT command must be executed to specify the format. The following example sets the DBID and restores the server parameter file using a control file autobackup in a non-default location.

```
SET DBID 348745982;
RUN
{
SET CONTROLFILE AUTOBACKUP FORMAT
FOR DEVICE TYPE DISK TO 'autobackup_format';
RESTORE SPFILE FROM AUTOBACKUP;
}
```

Recovering from the loss of a control file

The control file is critical to recovery of an Oracle database and so backing it up is of paramount importance. There are numerous ways to back up the control file. If you are using RMAN as your backup tool, the easiest of these is simply to configure RMAN to automatically back up the control file and server parameter file whenever a backup record is added. The autobackup feature is enabled and disabled as follows:

```
CONFIGURE CONTROLFILE AUTOBACKUP ON;
```

Even if CONTROLFILE AUTOBACKUP is not enabled, performing a whole database backup in RMAN will include a copy of the control file. The RMAN command BACKUP DATABASE is used to perform a whole database backup.

```
BACKUP DATABASE;
```

Outside of RMAN, there are two ALTER DATABASE commands that can be used to back up a control file. You can back up the control file to a binary file using the following statement:

```
ALTER DATABASE BACKUP CONTROLFILE TO '/oracle/backup/control.bkp';
```

Alternately, the following command writes a SQL script to a trace file that can be used to reproduce the control file. The alert log will contain the name and location of the trace file.

```
ALTER DATABASE BACKUP CONTROLFILE TO TRACE;
```

Finally, for a user managed backup while the database is shut down, you can use operating system commands to copy the control file.

Recovering the Database with a Backup Control File

In a recovery scenario where all copies of the current control file are lost or damaged, then you must restore and mount a backup control file. Copy the backup control file to all of the locations listed in the CONTROL_FILES initialization parameter. After the files are in place, the RECOVER command must be issued, even if no datafiles have been restored.

```
RECOVER DATABASE USING BACKUP CONTROLFILE UNTIL CANCEL;
```

Once the restore operation has been completed, open the database with the RESETLOGS option.

Recovering from the loss of Redo Log files

If all members of an online redo log group are damaged, the recovery process depends on the type of online redo log group affected and the whether or not the database is in archivelog mode. If the damaged online redo log group is current and active, then it is needed for crash recovery; otherwise, it is not. You can determine the status of the group associated with the damage files from V$LOGFILE:

```
SELECT group#, status, member
FROM   v$logfile;

GROUP#     STATUS        MEMBER
-------    -----------   ---------------------
0001                      /oracle/dbs/log1a.f
0001                      /oracle/dbs/log1b.f
0002       INVALID        /oracle/dbs/log2a.f
0002       INVALID        /oracle/dbs/log2b.f
0003                      /oracle/dbs/log3a.f
0003                      /oracle/dbs/log3b.f
```

You can determine which groups are active from the V$LOG view:

```
SELECT group#, status, archived
FROM   v$log;

GROUP#  STATUS     ARCHIVED
------  ---------  -----------
 0001   INACTIVE   YES
 0002   ACTIVE     NO
 0003   CURRENT    NO
```

If all members of an inactive online redo log group are damaged, then the procedure depends on whether it is possible to repair the media problem that damaged the group. If the failure is transient, then fix the problem.

The log writer will reuse the redo log group when required. For permanent failures, the damaged redo log group will halt normal database operation when the database tries to use it. The damaged group must be reinitialized manually by issuing the ALTER DATABASE CLEAR LOGFILE statement.

If all members of an active (but not current) log group are damaged and the database is still running, issue the ALTER SYSTEM CHECKPOINT statement. If the checkpoint is successful, then the redo log group will become inactive. At this point you can follow the steps for an inactive online redo log group. If the checkpoint is unsuccessful, or the database has halted, then depending on the archiving mode you must follow the recovery procedures corresponding to the current log group.

The current log group is the one LGWR is currently writing to. If a LGWR I/O operation fails, then LGWR terminates and the instance is terminated. In this case, you must restore a backup, perform incomplete recovery, and open the database with the RESETLOGS option.

Recovering from the Loss of Active Logs in NOARCHIVELOG Mode

If the media failure is temporary, then correct the problem so that the database can reuse the group when required.

- Restore the database from a consistent, whole database backup (data files and control files).
- Mount the database:
- To allow the database to reset the online redo logs, you must first mimic incomplete recovery:

```
RECOVER DATABASE UNTIL CANCEL
CANCEL
```

- Open the database using the RESETLOGS option:

```
ALTER DATABASE OPEN RESETLOGS;
```

- Shut down the database consistently.

```
SHUTDOWN IMMEDIATE
```

- Make a whole database backup.

Recovering from Loss of Active Logs in ARCHIVELOG Mode

- Begin incomplete media recovery, recovering up through the log before the damaged log.
- Ensure that the current name of the lost redo log can be used for a newly created file. If not, then rename the members of the damaged online redo log group to a new location.
- Open the database using the RESETLOGS option:

```
ALTER DATABASE OPEN RESETLOGS;
```

Perform table recovery from backups

It is now possible to use RMAN backups to recover a single table or table partition without affecting the remaining data in the database. In order for this to be possible, you must have a full backup of the SYSTEM, SYSAUX, and UNDO tablespaces, the SYSEXT tablespace if one exists plus the tablespace containing the table or table partition to be recovered. This can be very useful when a small number of tables need to recovered without affecting the entire database and Flashback table is not possible for one of the following reasons:

- The desired point-in-time is older than available undo.
- Data was lost after a TRUNCATE or a DDL operation that modified the structure of tables.

When recovering tables and table partitions using an RMAN backup, the following information must be provided:

- The name(s) of the table or table partition that must be recovered.
- The point in time the data should be recovered to.
- Whether the recovered tables or table partitions must be imported into the target database.

This information allows RMAN to automate the process of recovering the specified objects. When performing a table recovery, RMAN creates an auxiliary database. This database is then used as a temporary container to recover the supplied tables to the specified point in time. The steps performed by RMAN during a table recovery are:

1. It determines which backup contains the tables or table partitions that need to be recovered.
2. An auxiliary database is created and the specified tables or table partitions are recovered into it until the specified point in time.
3. A Data Pump export dump file that contains the recovered tables or table partitions is generated from the auxiliary database.
4. Optionally, the dump file is imported into the target instance. If the dump file is not imported as part of the recovery process, it must be manually imported later using the Data Pump Import utility.
5. Optionally, the recovered tables or table partitions are renamed in the target database.

Perform recovery of index and read only tablespaces, temp file

The common factor between a read only tablespace, a temporary tablespace and a tablespace that contains *only* indexes is that all three can be recovered without the application of redo. The specifics of why this is the case for each differs:

- A temporary tablespace never requires redo to be applied.
- A read-only tablespace generates no redo after being set to read-only.
- An index tablespace generates redo, but the information can be re-created without the application of redo logs.

Index Tablespace

A tablespace that contains only indexes will generate redo and be treated by RMAN just as any other writeable tablespace. Normally if there is damage to one of the datafiles, it is recovered in the same fashion as a tablespace that contains tables. However, because the information required to rebuild indexes is contained in their source table and the metadata in the data dictionary, it is possible to recover from the loss of an index tablespace even when there are no backups of the datafile or redo logs available. In order for this to work, it is required that no segments be in the tablespace except those for indexes. This can be determined by querying the DBA_SEGMENTS view:

```
SELECT owner, segment_name, segment_type
FROM   dba_segments
WHERE  tablespace_name = 'INDEX_TS'
AND    segment_type != 'INDEX';
```

To recreate the index tablespace, perform the following steps:

1. Take the damaged tablespace offline (if it is not already).

   ```
   ALTER TABLESPACE index_ts OFFLINE;
   ```

2. Use Oracle Data Pump to extract the metadata to create indexes and generate a SQL script.

   ```
   expdp username/password DIRECTORY=datadump
         DUMPFILE=indexes.dmp INCLUDE=index
   impdp username/password DIRECTORY=datadump
         DUMPFILE=indexes.dmp SQLFILE=indexes.sql
   ```

3. Drop the tablespace and delete its datafiles.

```
DROP TABLESPACE index_ts INCLUDING CONTENTS AND DATAFILES;
```

4. Create a new tablespace.

```
CREATE TABLESPACE index_ts DATAFILE
   '/u01/app/oracle/oradata/ocpdb/index01.dbf' size 100m;
```

5. Use the script from Step 2 to recreate the indexes.

Read Only Tablespaces

The primary purpose of read-only tablespaces is to optimize backup operations. Once a table has been made read-only and a single backup made after that point, RMAN no longer needs to create additional backups of the data files. If one or more datafiles of a read-only tablespace are lost or corrupted, recovery is simply a matter of restoring the backed up files. The database can remain online and there is no need for media recovery. The following steps will recover the datafiles and bring the tablespace back online:

1. Copy the datafile(s) back using OS utilities.

```
$ cp /backup/ocp_ro_ts01.dbf
  $ORACLE_HOME/oradata/ocpdb_1/ocp_ro_ts01.dbf
```

2. Connect to the database from SQL*Plus and bring the tablespace back online.

```
ALTER TABLESPACE ocp_ro ONLINE;
```

Temporary Tablespace

If one of more files belonging to the temporary tablespace is lost, any SQL statements that require space in the temporary tablespace will generate an error. If the database is up and you would like to recreate the file immediately, you can do so by creating a new datafile and dropping the old one as follows:

```
SQL> ALTER TABLESPACE temp ADD TEMPFILE
'/u01/app/oracle/oradata/orcl/temp02.dbf' SIZE 50M;
SQL> ALTER TABLESPACE temp DROP TEMPFILE
'/u01/app/oracle/oradata/orcl/temp01.dbf';
```

If the loss or damage to the datafile occurred while the database is down, simply starting the instance will automatically recreate the datafile. If Oracle detects a missing datafile on startup, it will issue the commands to recreate it. You will see a message in the alert log such are:

```
Re-creating tempfile /u01/app/oracle/oradata/orcl/temp01.dbf
```

If the file damage occurred while the database is started, but you would prefer to have the recovery done automatically (and assuming that restarting the database is an option), then shutting down and restarting the instance will recreate the file.

Restore a database to a new host

Restoring a database to a new host is a procedure that is used either to test out disaster recovery procedures or to permanently move a database to a new host. It is not the method that should be used to create a copy of an existing database. Restoring a database to a new host will result in a database with the same DBID as the original. When creating a copy of an existing database, the DUPLICATE command should be utilized. An RMAN DUPLICATE operation will assign a new DBID to the database it creates, allowing it to be registered in the same recovery catalog as the original database.

There are several steps to prepare for the restoration:

- Record the DBID of source database.
- Copy the source database initialization parameter file to the new host using OS commands.
- Ensure that RMAN is not connected to the recovery catalog. Otherwise, metadata about the restored data files will be stored in the recovery catalog which will interfere with future attempts to restore and recover the primary database.
- Ensure that backups used for the restore operation are accessible on the restore host.
- If this is a trial restore of the production database, then perform one of the following actions:
- If the fast recovery area of the new database is in a different location from the source, set DB_RECOVERY_FILE_DEST to the new location.
- If the fast recovery area will be the same physical location as the production database, set DB_UNIQUE_NAME in the test database instance to be different from the source database.

Once the above steps are completed, the disk backups must be restored to the new host. If the database will be moved to the new host using data file copies or backup sets on disk, the files must be transferred files manually to the new host:

1. Start RMAN and connect to a target database and recovery catalog.
2. Run a LIST command to see a listing of backups of the data file and control file autobackups.
3. Copy the backups to the new host with an operating system utility.

The steps to restore the database on a new host are:

1. Ensure that the backups from the above steps are accessible on the new host.

2. Configure the ORACLE_SID on the new host.

```
% setenv ORACLE_SID ocpdb2
```

3. Start RMAN on the new host and connect to the target database without connecting to the recovery catalog.

```
% rman NOCATALOG
RMAN> CONNECT TARGET /
```

4. Set the DBID and start the database instance without mounting the database.

```
SET DBID 1470242087;
STARTUP NOMOUNT
```

5. Restore and edit the server parameter file. Assuming the control file autobackup feature was enabled, the server parameter file is included in the backup. Allocate a channel to the media manager and restore the server parameter file:

```
RUN
{
ALLOCATE CHANNEL c1 DEVICE TYPE sbt PARMS '...';
SET CONTROLFILE AUTOBACKUP FORMAT FOR DEVICE TYPE DISK TO
'/tmp/%F';
RESTORE SPFILE
TO PFILE '?/oradata/test/initocpdb2.ora'
FROM AUTOBACKUP;
SHUTDOWN ABORT;
}
```

6. Edit the restored initialization parameter file to correct any location-specific parameters.
7. Restart the instance with the edited initialization parameter file.

```
STARTUP FORCE NOMOUNT
    PFILE='?/oradata/test/initocpdb2.ora';
```

8. Restore the control file from an autobackup and then mount the database.

```
RUN
{
ALLOCATE CHANNEL c1 DEVICE TYPE sbt PARMS '...';
RESTORE CONTROLFILE FROM AUTOBACKUP;
ALTER DATABASE MOUNT;
}
```

9. Catalog the data file copies using their new file names:

   ```
   CATALOG START WITH '/oracle/oradata/ocpdb2/';
   ```

   Alternately, specify files individually:

   ```
   CATALOG DATAFILECOPY
   '/oracle/oradata/ocpdb2/system01.dbf',
   '/oracle/oradata/ocpdb2/undotbs01.dbf',
   '/oracle/oradata/ocpdb2/tools01.dbf',
   '/oracle/oradata/ocpdb2t/users01.dbf';
   ```

10. Start a SQL*Plus session on the new database and query the database file names recorded in the control file. The recorded file names will be what existed on the original host. You can query V$ views to obtain this information:

    ```
    SPOOL LOG '/tmp/ocpdb2_dbfiles.out'
    SELECT file# AS "File/Grp#", name
    FROM   v$datafile
    UNION
    SELECT group#, member
    FROM   v$logfile;
    SPOOL OFF
    EXIT
    ```

11. Create an RMAN restore and recovery script. It must include the following steps:
    a. For each data file that is restored to a different path than it had on the source host, a SET NEWNAME command must be used to specify the new path.
    b. For each online redo log that will be created at a different location, the SQL ALTER DATABASE RENAME FILE command must be used to specify the path name on the destination host.
    c. Perform a SET UNTIL operation to limit recovery to the end of the archived redo logs.
    d. Restore and recover the database.

   e. Run the SWITCH DATAFILE ALL command so that the control file recognizes the new path names as the official new names of the data files.

12. The following example RMAN script can perform the restore and recovery operation:

```
RUN
{
# allocate a channel to the tape device
ALLOCATE CHANNEL c1 DEVICE TYPE sbt PARMS '...';
# rename the data files and online redo logs
SET NEWNAME FOR DATAFILE 1 TO
'?/oradata/ocpdb2/system01.dbf';
SET NEWNAME FOR DATAFILE 2 TO
'?/oradata/ocpdb2/undotbs01.dbf';
SET NEWNAME FOR DATAFILE 7 TO '?/oradata/ocpdb2/tools01.dbf';
SET NEWNAME FOR DATAFILE 8 TO '?/oradata/ocpdb2/users01.dbf';
ALTER DATABASE RENAME FILE '/u03/oracle/dbs/redo01.log'
TO '?/oradata/ocpdb2/redo01.log';
ALTER DATABASE RENAME FILE '/u03/oracle/dbs/redo02.log'
TO '?/oradata/ocpdb2/redo02.log';
# Do a SET UNTIL to prevent recovery of the online logs
SET UNTIL SCN 234567;
# restore the database and switch the data file names
RESTORE DATABASE;
SWITCH DATAFILE ALL;
# recover the database
RECOVER DATABASE;
}
EXIT
```

13. Execute the script created in the previous step.

```
% rman TARGET / NOCATALOG
RMAN> @ocpdb2_test.rman
```

14. Open the restored database with the RESETLOGS option.

```
ALTER DATABASE OPEN RESETLOGS;
```

Using Oracle Secure Backup

Configure and use Oracle Secure Backup

Oracle Secure Backup is a media manager solution from Oracle. It serves as a media management layer for RMAN through the SBT interface. Oracle Secure Backup is designed to protect data as it is backed up through the file system to tape. It supports major tape drives and tape libraries in SAN, Gigabit Ethernet, and SCSI environments. The Oracle Secure Backup Cloud Module can also provide integrated Oracle Database backup to third-party cloud storage. Oracle Secure Backup comes in two editions:

- **Oracle Secure Backup** -- This version supports distributed environments consisting of multiple servers. It provides advanced data protection requirements including encryption, rotation of tapes between multiple locations, and protection of NAS devices.
- **Oracle Secure Backup Express** -- This edition is available free with the Oracle Database. It is the same core product, but the Express edition is limited to a single host with one direct-attached tape drive. It also has some restrictions on the usage of advanced features.

There is also the Oracle Secure Backup Cloud Module. This is independent of the Oracle Secure Backup tape management editions. The cloud module provides Oracle Database backup to cloud storage using Recovery Manager (RMAN). It can be used in addition to the Oracle Secure Backup tape management solution or other third-party media-management products.

The basic steps to configure Oracle Secure Backup for use with RMAN follow. For more details on these steps, read the Oracle Secure Backup Installation and Configuration Guide.

1. Configure RMAN access to the Oracle Secure Backup SBT.
2. Create an Oracle Secure Backup user preauthorized for RMAN operations.

3. Create media families for data files and archived redo logs. This is optional, but recommended. If no media families are created, the RMAN-DEFAULT media family will be used.
4. Optionally, configure database backup storage selectors or RMAN media management parameters.

In order for Oracle Secure Backup to honor SBT requests, the user making the request must be preauthorized for RMAN backup on that host. The preauthorized Oracle Secure Backup user must meet two sets of requirements.

- The user must be mapped to operating system privileges that allow them to access the files to be backed up or restored.
- The user must be assigned to an Oracle Secure Backup class possessing the rights to access Oracle backups (set to owner, class, or all) and to perform Oracle backups and restores.

Only a single Oracle Secure Backup user can be preauthorized on a particular host. It is possible to have multiple RMAN users who can start backup or restore operations. It is also possible to preauthorize an Oracle Secure Backup user for command-line (obtool) operations. Users with this capability can utilize backup and restore scripts. It is possible to configure a preauthorized user during installation of the Oracle Secure Backup software. After installation a user can be configured using either the Oracle Secure Backup Web tool or the mkuser command in obtool.

Using Flashback Technologies

Describe the Flashback technologies

Configure a database to use Flashback technologies

There are a number of different capabilities that Oracle includes under the 'Flashback' umbrella. The methods used to implement them likewise make use of several different technologies. The common factor of all the Oracle Flashback features is that they allow database administrators to either view data as it existed at a previous point in time or to change data in the database to match what existed at an earlier point in time. That said, the various Flashback technologies and how to configure them for use follow

Flashback Table

By default, when a table is dropped, the database does not immediately remove the space associated with the table. Instead, the database renames it and places the table and any associated objects that were dropped in a recycle bin. If it is determined that the table was dropped in error, it can be recovered at a later date. The FLASHBACK TABLE statement is used to restore the table.

The recycle bin is a data dictionary table that contains information required to recover dropped objects. The dropped objects themselves remain where they were before being dropped and still occupy the same amount of disk space. Dropped objects also continue to count against user space quotas until they are explicitly purged or are purged by the database due to tablespace space constraints. The Oracle recycle bin is enabled by default, so there is no configuration required to use this feature.

Flashback Query

Flashback Query, Flashback Version Query and Flashback Transaction Query all make use of undo records to show data as it existed in the past. Flashback Transaction Query also gives information about transactions that have altered data. Oracle databases will always have an undo tablespace, so these features can be used without any configuration. The size of the undo tablespace will affect how far back in time it is possible to view data and transactions. The next chapter on undo retention will deal more with that.

Flashback Database

Oracle's Flashback Database feature allows you to set the database back to an earlier time in order to correct problems caused by logical data corruption or user errors within a designated time window. Flashback Database is much more efficient than performing a point-in-time recovery and does not require a backup and restore operation. Flashback Database is accessible through the RMAN command FLASHBACK DATABASE or the SQL statement FLASHBACK DATABASE.

To enable Flashback Database, the database must have a Fast Recovery Area configured and a flashback retention target set. This target specifies how far in the past it should possible to rewind the database. Flashback Database uses its own logging mechanism, creating flashback logs and storing them in the fast recovery area. The database must be set up in advance to create flashback logs in order to take advantage of this feature. Once configured, at regular intervals, the database copies images of each altered block in every data file into the flashback logs. These block images can later be used to reconstruct the data file contents to any moment for which logs exist. In addition to the flashback logs, redo logs on disk or tape must be available for the entire time period spanned by the flashback logs. The range of SCNs for which there is currently enough flashback log data to support the FLASHBACK DATABASE command is called the flashback database window.

If the Fast Recovery Area does not contain sufficient space for recovery files such as archived redo logs and other backups needed for the retention policy, the database may delete the flashback logs starting from the earliest SCNs. The flashback retention target does not guarantee that Flashback Database is available for the full period. A larger Fast Recovery Area may be required in this case.

Guarantee undo retention

Any time that automatic undo management is enabled, there is an undo retention period. This is the minimum amount of time that the database will try to keep old undo information from being overwritten. The undo retention period is based on the undo tablespace size and system activity. It is possible to use the UNDO_RETENTION initialization parameter to specify a minimum undo retention period.

It the undo tablespace is fixed size, the value of UNDO_RETENTION is ignored. The database automatically uses system activity and undo tablespace size to tune the undo retention period for the best possible retention. For an undo tablespace set to AUTOEXTEND, the database will attempt to honor the specified UNDO_RETENTION period. When space is low, the tablespace will auto-extend (up to the MAXSIZE) instead of overwriting unexpired undo information. If the MAXSIZE is reached, the database may not be able to meet the UNDO_RETENTION value. The minimum undo retention period (in seconds) can be set in two ways:

- Set UNDO_RETENTION in the initialization parameter file.

```
UNDO_RETENTION = 2000
```

- The UNDO_RETENTION value can be modified dynamically using the ALTER SYSTEM statement.

```
ALTER SYSTEM SET UNDO_RETENTION = 3000;
```

The effect of an UNDO_RETENTION parameter change can only be honored if the current undo tablespace has sufficient space.

When using a fixed-size undo tablespace, the Undo Advisor is valuable for estimating the optimum size. It can be accessed through Oracle Enterprise Manager Express or through DBMS_ADVISOR. The Undo Advisor uses AWR data to create its analysis, so there must be sufficient workload statistics available for it to make accurate recommendations. When using the Undo Advisor, two values must be estimated:

- The length of the expected longest running query.
- The longest interval required for Oracle Flashback operations

The larger of these two values is used as input to the Undo Advisor. The Undo Advisor does not alter the size of the undo tablespace, it only offers a recommended size. You must use ALTER DATABASE statements to change the tablespace data file size. The following example changes an undo tablespace with a file called undotbs.dbf to a fixed size of 400MB.

```
ALTER DATABASE DATAFILE '/u01/oracle/dbs/undotbs.dbf' RESIZE 400M;
ALTER DATABASE DATAFILE '/u01/oracle/dbs/undotbs.dbf' AUTOEXTEND OFF;
```

The RETENTION_GUARANTEE clause is used to guarantee the success of long-running queries or Oracle Flashback operations. When enabled, the specified minimum undo retention is guaranteed. Oracle will never overwrite unexpired undo data even when doing so means that transactions fail from lack of space in the undo tablespace. When retention guarantee is disabled (the default), the database can overwrite unexpired undo when space is low. The RETENTION GUARANTEE clause can be specified for an undo tablespace at create time with either the

CREATE DATABASE or CREATE UNDO TABLESPACE statement. The clause can be used to modify an existing tablespace using the ALTER TABLESPACE statement. Retention guarantee is disabled with the RETENTION NOGUARANTEE clause.

Use Flashback to query data

Use Flashback Query

Oracle Flashback Query allows a prior time to be specified when executing a query against the database. The query will return results as they would have appeared at that time. This can be used to recover from an unwanted change in the recent past by selecting a target time before the error and executing a query to retrieve the lost or damaged data.

The Oracle Flashback Query capability is implemented via the AS OF clause in a SELECT statement. When the AS OF clause is included, Oracle retrieves data as it existed at an earlier point in time. The AS OF clause must explicitly reference a past time through a time stamp or System Change Number (SCN). When a timestamp is used, the time will be accurate to within three seconds. If greater accuracy is required, an SCN should be utilized. The query will return committed data that was current at the specified time/SCN. The following example retrieves the row for employee with the ID 107 at an earlier point in time:

```
SELECT *
FROM   hr.employees
AS OF TIMESTAMP
    TO_TIMESTAMP('2014-03-14 12:30:00', 'YYYY-MM-DD HH:MI:SS')
WHERE employee_id = 107;
```

If that record had been accidentally deleted from the table, it could be recovered with the following statement:

```
INSERT INTO hr.employees
(SELECT *
 FROM   hr.employees
 AS OF TIMESTAMP
     TO_TIMESTAMP('2014-03-14 12:30:00', 'YYYY-MM-DD HH:MI:SS')
 WHERE employee_id = 107);
```

Use Flashback Version Query

Flashback Version Query is used to retrieve metadata and historical data for a specific interval. The interval can be specified by two timestamps or by two SCNs. The metadata returned includes the start and end time a version existed, type of DML operation used to create it, and the identity of the transaction that created each row version. The VERSIONS BETWEEN clause of a SELECT statement is used to generate a Flashback Version Query. The syntax of the VERSIONS BETWEEN clause is: VERSIONS {BETWEEN {SCN | TIMESTAMP} start AND end}.

The pseudocolumns returned by a Flashback version query are:

- **VERSIONS_START[SCN/TIME]** -- Starting System Change Number (SCN) or TIMESTAMP when the row version was created. NULL if version is from before the start value.
- **VERSIONS_END[SCN/TIME]** -- SCN or TIMESTAMP when the row version expired. If NULL, then either the row version was current at the time of the query or the row is for a DELETE operation.
- **VERSIONS_XID** -- Identifier of the transaction that created the row version.
- **VERSIONS_OPERATION** -- Operation performed by the transaction: I for insertion, D for deletion, or U for update. The version is that of the row that was inserted, deleted, or updated.

A given row version is valid starting at VERSIONS_START* up to, but not including, VERSIONS_END*. That is, it is valid for any time 't' such that VERSIONS_START* <= t < VERSIONS_END*. The following three updates were issued against the EMPLOYEES table, with a pause in-between.

```
UPDATE employees SET salary = 97000
WHERE emp_last='McCoy';
UPDATE employees SET salary = 102000
WHERE emp_last='McCoy';
UPDATE employees SET salary = 105000
WHERE emp_last='McCoy';
COMMIT;
```

Then the following Flashback Versions query was run against employees:

```
SELECT versions_starttime, versions_endtime,
       versions_xid, versions_operation AS OP,
       salary
  FROM employees
  VERSIONS BETWEEN TIMESTAMP
      TO_TIMESTAMP('22-FEB-14 11.46.00PM','DD-MON-YY HH:MI:SSAM')
  AND TO_TIMESTAMP('22-FEB-14 11.52.00PM','DD-MON-YY HH:MI:SSAM')
  WHERE emp_last = 'McCoy';
```

```
VERSIONS_STARTTIME    VERSIONS_ENDTIME      VERSIONS_XID     OP SALARY
-------------------- --------------------- ---------------- -- ------
22-FEB-14 11.51.08PM                       09000900A9010000 U  105000
22-FEB-14 11.49.50PM 22-FEB-14 11.51.08PM 04001A003F010000 U  102000
22-FEB-14 11.49.02PM 22-FEB-14 11.49.50PM 03002100A2010000 U   97000
                     22-FEB-14 11.49.02PM                       93500
```

From the results above, you see the three updates against the table, each increasing the salary column value. It's clear when each salary value started and ended (save the initial value for which the start time was outside the window, and the final value which is current (and therefore has no end time). You can use VERSIONS_XID with Oracle Flashback Transaction Query to locate the metadata for any of the three transactions. This will include the SQL required to undo the row change and the user responsible for the change.

Use Flashback Transaction Query

Oracle Flashback Transaction allows a transaction to be reversed. Oracle will determine the dependencies between transactions and create a compensating transaction to reverse the unwanted change. The result is a state as if the transaction and any dependent transactions had never happened.

A Flashback Transaction Query is used to retrieve metadata and historical data for a single transaction or for all transactions in a supplied interval. The data is generated from the static data dictionary view FLASHBACK_TRANSACTION_QUERY. The Flashback Transaction Query creates a column UNDO_SQL. The SQL text in this field is the logical opposite of the DML operation performed by the transaction shown. The code from this field can usually reverse the original transaction within reason (e.g. a SQL_UNDO INSERT operation would be unlikely to insert a row back at the same ROWID from which it was deleted). As a general rule, Oracle Flashback Transaction Query is used in conjunction with an Oracle Flashback Version Query that provides transaction IDs.

```
SELECT operation, start_scn, commit_scn, logon_user
  FROM flashback_transaction_query
    WHERE xid = HEXTORAW('09000900A9010000');

OPERATION     START_SCN COMMIT_SCN LOGON_USER
------------ --------- ---------- ------------
UNKNOWN         393394     393463 OCPGURU
BEGIN           393394     393463 OCPGURU
```

The following statement uses Oracle Flashback Version Query as a subquery to associate each row version with the LOGON_USER responsible for the row data change.

```
SELECT xid, logon_user
  FROM flashback_transaction_query
    WHERE xid IN (
      SELECT versions_xid
      FROM employees VERSIONS BETWEEN TIMESTAMP
        TO_TIMESTAMP('22-FEB-14 11.40.00 PM',
                     'DD-MON-YY HH:MI:SS AM') AND
        TO_TIMESTAMP('22-FEB-14 11.56.00 PM',
                     'DD-MON-YY HH:MI:SS AM') );
```

You can use the DBMS_FLASHBACK.TRANSACTION_BACKOUT procedure to roll back a transaction and its dependent transactions while the database remains online. Transaction backout uses undo data to create and execute the compensating transactions to return the affected data to its original state. TRANSACTION_BACKOUT does not commit the DML operations that it performs as part of transaction backout. However, it does hold all the required locks on rows and tables in the right form to prevent other dependencies from entering the system. To make the transaction backout permanent, you must explicitly commit the transaction.

In order to configure a database for the Oracle Flashback Transaction Query feature, the database must be running in ARCHIVELOG mode. In addition, the database administrator must enable supplemental logging.

```
ALTER DATABASE ADD SUPPLEMENTAL LOG DATA;
```

To perform Oracle Flashback Query operations, the administrator must grant appropriate privileges to the user who will be performing them. For Oracle Flashback Query, the administrator can do either of the following:

- To allow access to specific objects during queries, grant FLASHBACK and SELECT privileges on those objects.
- To allow queries on all tables, grant the FLASHBACK ANY TABLE privilege.

For Oracle Flashback Transaction Query, the administrator will need to grant the SELECT ANY TRANSACTION privilege. To allow execution of undo SQL code retrieved by an Oracle Flashback Transaction, the administrator will need to grant: SELECT, UPDATE, DELETE, and INSERT privileges for the appropriate tables. Finally, the administrator will need to grant the user EXECUTE privileges on the DBMS_FLASHBACK Package.

Flash back a transaction

The following example updates a record in the AIRCRAFT_FLIGHTS table. It then locates the transaction ID using a Flashback versions query. The transaction ID can be used to locate the SQL required to undo the transaction from the UNDO_SQL column of a Flashback Transaction Query. The text in the UNDO_SQL column is then executed to reverse the original transaction.

```
UPDATE aircraft_flights
SET    flight_id = 'Flight 081109'
WHERE  flt_id = 1600;
1 rows updated.

SELECT versions_xid, versions_operation AS OP, flight_id
  FROM aircraft_flights
  VERSIONS BETWEEN TIMESTAMP
      TO_TIMESTAMP('26-MAY-15 11.03.00PM','DD-MON-YY HH:MI:SSAM')
  AND TO_TIMESTAMP('26-MAY-15 11.05.00PM','DD-MON-YY HH:MI:SSAM')
  WHERE flt_id = 1600;

VERSIONS_XID     OP FLIGHT_ID
---------------- -- -------------
02001F0034030010 U  Flight 081109


SELECT undo_sql
  FROM flashback_transaction_query
    WHERE xid = HEXTORAW('02001F0034030010');

UNDO_SQL
---------------------------------------------------------
update "OCPGURU"."AIRCRAFT_FLIGHTS" set "FLIGHT_ID" =
'Flight 081108' where ROWID = 'AAALRXAAEAAABLhABX';


update "OCPGURU"."AIRCRAFT_FLIGHTS"
set "FLIGHT_ID" = 'Flight 081108'
where ROWID = 'AAALRXAAEAAABLhABX';
1 rows updated.
```

Perform Flashback Table operations

Perform Flashback Table

By default, when a table is dropped, the database does not immediately remove the space associated with the table. Instead, the database renames it and places the table and any associated objects that were dropped in a recycle bin. If it is determined that the table was dropped in error, it can be recovered at a later date. The FLASHBACK TABLE statement can be used to restore the table.

The recycle bin is a data dictionary table that contains information required to recover dropped objects. The dropped objects themselves remain where they were before being dropped and still occupy the same amount of disk space. Dropped objects also continue to count against user space quotas until they are explicitly purged or are purged by the database due to tablespace space constraints.

When a tablespace including its contents is dropped, the recycle bin does not come into play. The storage where the objects were no longer exists. The database purges any entries in the recycle bin for objects that were located in the tablespace. If the recycle bin is disabled, dropped tables and their dependent objects are simply dropped. They must be recovered by other means, such as recovering from backup. The recycle bin is enabled by default.

The FLASHBACK TABLE ... TO BEFORE DROP statement is used to recover objects from the recycle bin. When recovering a table, you must specify either the system-generated name of the table in the recycle bin or the original table name. An optional RENAME TO clause lets you rename the table as you recover it. The USER_RECYCLEBIN view can be used to obtain the system-generated name. To use the FLASHBACK TABLE ... TO BEFORE DROP statement, you need the same privileges required to drop the table.

Restore tables from the recycle bin

The following example creates a test table, FB_DROP_TEST, drops it, and then restores it using the FLASHBACK TABLE capability.

```
CREATE TABLE fb_drop_test (
col1    NUMBER);
table FB_DROP_TEST created.

INSERT INTO fb_drop_test VALUES (1);
1 rows inserted.

DROP TABLE fb_drop_test;
table FB_DROP_TEST dropped.

SELECT * FROM fb_drop_test;
Error report -
SQL Error: ORA-00942: table or view does not exist
00942. 00000 -  "table or view does not exist"

FLASHBACK TABLE fb_drop_test TO BEFORE DROP;
table FB_DROP_TEST succeeded.

SELECT * FROM fb_drop_test;
      COL1
----------
         1
```

When performing the FLASHBACK TABLE operation, it is possible to rename the table. This might be used if a new table has already been created with the same name since the original was dropped. The following example demonstrates using the RENAME option:

```
DROP TABLE fb_drop_test;
table FB_DROP_TEST dropped.

FLASHBACK TABLE fb_drop_test TO BEFORE DROP
RENAME TO fb_drop_test2;
table FB_DROP_TEST succeeded.

SELECT * FROM fb_drop_test2;
      COL1
----------
         1
```

Describe and use Flashback Data Archive

Use Flashback Data Archive

Oracle's Flashback Data Archive feature allows you to store table-level change history for extended periods of time. It provides the ability to track all transactional changes to a table over its lifetime. The Flashback Data Archive functionality is useful to maintain compliance with record storage policies and audit reports. It is possible to have multiple Flashback Data Archives in a single database, one of which can be (although it is not required), specified as the default for the database. Each Flashback Data Archive in a database is configured with a retention time that determines how long data stored in that particular archive is to be retained.

Flashback archiving is off for any table by default. You can enable flashback archiving for a table if all of the following are true:

- You have the FLASHBACK ARCHIVE object privilege on the Flashback Data Archive that you want to use for that table.
- The table you want to archive is not nested, clustered, temporary, remote, or external.
- The table does not contain LONG or nested columns.

Once flashback archiving is enabled for a table, you can disable it only if you either have the FLASHBACK ARCHIVE ADMINISTER system privilege or you are logged into the database with SYSDBA privileges. While flashback archiving is enabled for a table, some DDL statements are not allowed on it and will generate an ORA-55610 error. The following operations are disallowed:

- ALTER TABLE statement that includes an UPGRADE TABLE clause, with or without an INCLUDING DATA clause
- ALTER TABLE statement that moves or exchanges a partition or subpartition operation
- DROP TABLE statement

Flashback Data Archive can be the solution to any number of business requirements. Many government agencies and organizations require that data be kept for a set number of years before being deleted. The settings of a Flashback Data Archive can be specifically configured to meet these requirements. After the specified time period has expired, the data will automatically be aged out of the archive – effectively 'shredding' it without requiring direct intervention. It can help in satisfying some of the storage requirements for such legislative acts as Sarbanes-Oxley and HIPAA. It can provide a source of data for audits. Flashback data archive can also be used as a simple method to recover accidentally altered or deleted data.

A Flashback Data Archive is created using the CREATE FLASHBACK ARCHIVE statement. If you are logged on with SYSDBA privileges, you can also specify that this is the default Flashback Data Archive for the system. When creating a new flashback data archive, you must specify the following:

- Name of the Flashback Data Archive
- Name of the first tablespace of the Flashback Data Archive
- Retention time (number of days that Flashback Data Archive data for the table is guaranteed to be stored)
- (Optional) Maximum amount of space that the Flashback Data Archive can use in the first tablespace. The default is unlimited.

Create a default Flashback Data Archive named fda1 using a maximum of 15 Gigs of tablespace fda_tbs1. The data will be retained for two years:

```
CREATE FLASHBACK ARCHIVE DEFAULT fda1
TABLESPACE fda_tbs1 QUOTA 15G RETENTION 2 YEAR;
```

Create a Flashback Data Archive named fda2 that uses tablespace fda_tbs2, whose data will be retained for three years:

```
CREATE FLASHBACK ARCHIVE fda2
TABLESPACE fda_tbs2 RETENTION 3 YEAR;
```

Using the ALTER FLASHBACK ARCHIVE statement, you can change the retention time of a Flashback Data Archive; purge some or all of its data; and add, modify, or remove tablespaces. If you are logged on with SYSDBA privileges, you can also make a specific archive the default Flashback Data Archive for the system.

- Make Flashback Data Archive fla1 the default Flashback Data Archive:

  ```
  ALTER FLASHBACK ARCHIVE fda1 SET DEFAULT;
  ```

- Add an additional 5Gigs quota of tablespace fda_tbs1 to Flashback Data Archive fda1:

  ```
  ALTER FLASHBACK ARCHIVE fda1
  ADD TABLESPACE da_tbs1 QUOTA 5G;
  ```

- Add unlimited quota on tablespace fda_tbs3 to Flashback Data Archive fda1:

  ```
  ALTER FLASHBACK ARCHIVE fda1 ADD TABLESPACE tbs3;
  ```

- Change the retention time for Flashback Data Archive fda1 to four years:

  ```
  ALTER FLASHBACK ARCHIVE fda1 MODIFY RETENTION 4 YEAR;
  ```

- Purge all historical data older than one day from Flashback Data Archive fda1:

  ```
  ALTER FLASHBACK ARCHIVE fda1
  PURGE BEFORE TIMESTAMP (SYSTIMESTAMP - INTERVAL '1' DAY);
  ```

You can drop a Flashback Data Archive with the DROP FLASHBACK ARCHIVE statement. This statement will delete its historical data, but will not drop the tablespace the archive was stored on. To remove Flashback Data Archive fda1 and all its historical data:

```
DROP FLASHBACK ARCHIVE fda1;
```

Flashback archiving is disabled for all tables by default. If a flashback data archive exists in the database, and you have the FLASHBACK ARCHIVE privilege on it, you can enable flashback archiving for a table. To enable flashback archiving for a table, you use the FLASHBACK ARCHIVE clause in either a CREATE TABLE or ALTER TABLE statement. It's possible to set the specific Flashback Data Archive where the data for the table will be stored in the FLASHBACK ARCHIVE clause. If no clause is provided, the default Flashback Data Archive for the database will be used. Some examples of making tables use flashback archiving are:

- Create table dept and use the default Flashback Data Archive:

```
CREATE TABLE dept (DEPTNO NUMBER(4) NOT NULL,
                   DEPTNAME VARCHAR2(10))
FLASHBACK ARCHIVE;
```

- Create table employee and use the Flashback Data Archive fda1:

```
CREATE TABLE dept (DEPTNO NUMBER(4) NOT NULL,
                   DEPTNAME VARCHAR2(10))
FLASHBACK ARCHIVE fda1;
```

- Enable flashback archiving for the table dept and use the default Flashback Data Archive:

```
ALTER TABLE dept FLASHBACK ARCHIVE;
```

- Enable flashback archiving for the table dept and use the Flashback Data Archive fda1:

```
ALTER TABLE dept FLASHBACK ARCHIVE fda1;
```

- Disable flashback archiving for the table dept:

```
ALTER TABLE dept NO FLASHBACK ARCHIVE;
```

The following views in the data dictionary are specific to the Flashback Data Archive:

- DBA_FLASHBACK_ARCHIVE_TABLES
- DBA_FLASHBACK_ARCHIVE
- DBA_FLASHBACK_ARCHIVE_TS

Use DBMS_FLASHBACK_ARCHIVE package

The DBMS_FLASHBACK_ARCHIVE package provides a number of subprograms that extend the functionality of the Flashback Data Archive functionality of Oracle. One of the more common uses is to allow DDL changes to be made to a table that has had flashback archive enabled. Once Flashback Data Archive has been enabled for a table, users are prevented from issuing any DDL statements on it. The following example will disassociate the DEPT table from its history table:

```
EXEC DBMS_FLASHBACK_ARCHIVE.DISASSOCIATE_FBA('HR','DEPT');
```

Once the above command has been executed, it is possible to make DDL changes to the DEPT table (for example adding a column) that would have generated an error because of the associated history table. Once the DDL has been completed, the following command will reassociate the table with its history table:

```
EXEC DBMS_FLASHBACK_ARCHIVE.REASSOCIATE_FBA('HR','DEPT')
```

There are a number of subprograms available in the DBMS_FLASHBACK_ARCHIVE package, including:

- **ADD_TABLE_TO_APPLICATION** -- Takes an application name and adds a table to the application as a security table.
- **CREATE_TEMP_HISTORY_TABLE** -- Creates a table called TEMP_HISTORY with the correct definition in schema.

- **DISABLE_APPLICATION** -- Takes an application name and marks a table in it as a security table.
- **DISABLE_ASOF_VALID_TIME** -- Disables session level valid-time flashback.
- **DISASSOCIATE_FBA** -- Disassociates the given table from the flashback data archive.
- **DROP_APPLICATION** -- Takes an application name and removes it from the list of applications.
- **ENABLE_APPLICATION** -- Takes an application name and enables Flashback Data Archive on all the security tables for this application.
- **ENABLE_AT_VALID_TIME** -- Enables session level valid time flashback.
- **EXTEND_MAPPINGS** -- Extends time mappings to times in the past.
- **GET_SYS_CONTEXT** -- Gets the context previously selected by the SET_CONTEXT_LEVEL Procedure.
- **IMPORT_HISTORY** -- Imports history from a table called TEMP_HISTORY in the given schema.
- **LOCK_DOWN_APPLICATION** -- Takes an application name and makes all the security tables read-only. The group called SYSTEM cannot be locked.
- **PURGE_CONTEXT** -- Purges the context to be saved selected by the SET_CONTEXT_LEVEL Procedure.
- **REASSOCIATE_FBA** -- Reassociates the given table with the flashback data archive.
- **REGISTER_APPLICATION** -- Takes an application name and optionally a Flashback Data Archive, and registers an application for database hardening.
- **REMOVE_TABLE_FROM_APPLICATION** -- Takes an application name and marks a table in it as no longer being a security table.
- **SET_CONTEXT_LEVEL** -- Defines how much of the user context is to be saved.

Using Flashback Database

Perform Flashback Database

Configure Flashback Database

Oracle's Flashback Database feature allows you to set the database back to an earlier time in order to correct problems caused by logical data corruption or user errors within a designated time window. Flashback Database is much more efficient than performing a point-in-time recovery and does not require a backup and restore operation. Flashback Database is accessible through the RMAN command FLASHBACK DATABASE or the SQL statement FLASHBACK DATABASE.

To enable Flashback Database, the database must have a Fast Recovery Area configured and a flashback retention target set. This target specifies how far in the past it should possible to rewind the database. Flashback Database uses its own logging mechanism, creating flashback logs and storing them in the fast recovery area. The database must be set up in advance to create flashback logs in order to take advantage of this feature. Once configured, at regular intervals, the database copies images of each altered block in every data file into the flashback logs. These block images can later be used to reconstruct the data file contents to any moment for which logs exist. In addition to the flashback logs, redo logs on disk or tape must be available for the entire time period spanned by the flashback logs. The range of SCNs for which there is currently enough flashback log data to support the FLASHBACK DATABASE command is called the flashback database window.

If the Fast Recovery Area does not contain sufficient space for recovery files such as archived redo logs and other backups needed for the retention policy, the database may delete the flashback logs starting from the earliest SCNs. The flashback retention target does <u>not</u> guarantee that Flashback Database is available for the full period. A larger Fast Recovery Area may be required in this case.

Flashback Database has the following limitations:

- It can only undo changes to a data file made by Oracle Database. It cannot be used to repair media failures, or recover from accidental deletion of data files.
- It cannot undo a shrink data file operation.
- If the database control file is restored from backup or re-created, all accumulated flashback log information is discarded.
- If you Flashback Database to a target time at which a NOLOGGING operation was in progress, block corruption is likely in the database objects and datafiles affected by the NOLOGGING operation.

A normal restore point simply assigns a restore point name to an SCN or specific point in time. It functions as an alias for this SCN. If you use flashback features or point-in-time recovery, the restore point name can be used instead of a time or SCN. Normal restore points eventually age out of the control file if not manually deleted, so they require no ongoing maintenance. The following commands support the use of restore points:

- RECOVER DATABASE and FLASHBACK DATABASE commands in RMAN
- FLASHBACK TABLE statement in SQL

A guaranteed restore point also serves as an alias for an SCN in recovery operations. However, guaranteed restore points never age out of the control file and must be explicitly dropped. It ensures that you can use Flashback Database to rewind a database to the restore point SCN, even if the generation of flashback logs is not enabled. When enabled, a guaranteed restore point enforces the retention of flashback logs all the way back in time to the guaranteed SCN.

In order to enable Flashback Database, you must first ensure the database instance is open or mounted. If the instance is mounted, then the database must be shut down cleanly unless it is a physical standby database.

1. Optionally, set the DB_FLASHBACK_RETENTION_TARGET to the length of the desired flashback window in minutes. The default is 1 day (1440 minutes).
2. Enable the Flashback Database feature for the whole database:

   ```
   ALTER DATABASE FLASHBACK ON;
   ```

3. Optionally, disable flashback logging for specific tablespaces.

To disable Flashback Database logging, you must issue the following command on a database instance that is either in mount or open state:

```
ALTER DATABASE FLASHBACK OFF;
```

Maintaining flashback logs does not impose significant overhead on a database instance. Changed blocks are written to the flashback logs at relatively infrequent, regular intervals, to limit processing and I/O overhead. Optimizing performance is primarily a matter of ensuring that the writes occur as fast as possible.

- Use a fast file system for your fast recovery area, preferably without operating system file caching.
- Configure enough disk spindles for the file system that holds the fast recovery area.
- If the storage system used to hold the fast recovery area does not have nonvolatile RAM, then try to configure the file system on striped storage volumes with a relatively small stripe size such as 128 KB.
- For large databases, set the initialization parameter LOG_BUFFER to at least 8 MB.

There are several database views that allow you to monitor the impact of flashback logs on the database. The V$FLASHBACK_DATABASE_LOG view allows you to monitor the Flashback Database retention target and how much space is being used by the flashback logs in the Fast Recovery Area.

- **OLDEST_FLASHBACK_SCN** -- Lowest system change number (SCN) in the flashback data, for any incarnation.
- **OLDEST_FLASHBACK_TIME** -- Time of the lowest SCN in the flashback data, for any incarnation.
- **RETENTION_TARGET** -- Target retention time (in minutes).
- **FLASHBACK_SIZE** -- Current size (in bytes) of the flashback data.
- **ESTIMATED_FLASHBACK_SIZE** -- Estimated size of flashback data needed for the current target retention.

The V$FLASHBACK_DATABASE_STAT view displays statistics for monitoring the I/O overhead of logging flashback data. It also displays the estimated flashback space needed based on previous workloads.

- **BEGIN_TIME** -- Beginning of the time interval.
- **END_TIME** -- End of the time interval.
- **FLASHBACK_DATA** -- Number of bytes of flashback data written during the interval.
- **DB_DATA** -- Number of bytes of database data read and written during the interval.
- **REDO_DATA** -- Number of bytes of redo data written during the interval.
- **ESTIMATED_FLASHBACK_SIZE** -- Value of ESTIMATED_FLASHBACK_SIZE in V$FLASHBACK_DATABASE_LOG at the end of the time interval.

The V$RECOVERY_FILE_DEST view displays information about the disk quota and current disk usage in the fast recovery area.

- **NAME** -- Location name. This is the value specified in the DB_RECOVERY_FILE_DEST initialization parameter.
- **SPACE_LIMIT** -- Maximum amount of disk space (in bytes) that the database can use for the fast recovery area. This is the value specified in the DB_RECOVERY_FILE_DEST_SIZE initialization parameter.

- **SPACE_USED** -- Amount of disk space (in bytes) used by fast recovery area files created in current and all previous fast recovery areas. Changing fast recovery areas does not reset SPACE_USED to 0.
- **SPACE_RECLAIMABLE** -- Total amount of disk space (in bytes) that can be created by deleting obsolete, redundant, and other low priority files from the fast recovery area.
- **NUMBER_OF_FILES** -- Number of files in the fast recovery area.

Perform Flashback Database

If a database has been configured for flashback logging as described in the previous section, it is possible use the FLASHBACK DATABASE command to return the database contents to points in time within the flashback window. The database must be mounted when the FLASHBACK DATABASE is issued. If restore points have been created for the database, they make flashback database operations simpler. However, they are not required. The steps to rewind a database with Flashback Database are:

1. Start RMAN and connect to a target database.
2. Ensure that the database is in a mounted state.

```
SHUTDOWN IMMEDIATE;
STARTUP MOUNT;
```

3. Run the FLASHBACK DATABASE command. Following are three different forms of the command:

```
FLASHBACK DATABASE TO SCN 571340;
FLASHBACK DATABASE TO RESTORE POINT GOOD_TIMES;
FLASHBACK DATABASE TO TIMESTAMP TO_DATE('28-MAY-2015
01:00:00',
                                                  'DD-MON-YYYY
HH24:MI:SS');
```

4. After performing the Flashback Database, open the database read-only in SQL*Plus and execute some queries to verify the database contents.

```
ALTER DATABASE OPEN READ ONLY;
```

5. Once satisfied with the results, issue the following sequence of commands to shut down and then open the database:

```
SHUTDOWN IMMEDIATE;
STARTUP MOUNT;
ALTER DATABASE OPEN RESETLOGS;
```

Transporting Data

Describe and use transportable tablespaces and databases

Transport tablespaces between databases using image copies or backup sets

It is possible to transport tablespaces between servers using RMAN's transport tablespace capability. The RMAN TRANSPORT TABLESPACE command will create a transportable tablespace set. This set contains data files for a one or more tablespaces plus an export file that contains the structural metadata for included tablespaces. The export file is generated by Data Pump Export rather than by RMAN. The RMAN TRANSPORT TABLESPACE command does not require access to the live data files from the tablespaces to be transported. It creates the tablespace set from database backups (either image copies or backup sets). It is also possible to specify a target point in time, SCN, or restore point for the set to be exported so long at that time exists within the recovery window.

In order to create a tablespace set with the TRANSPORT TABLESPACE operation, a backup of all needed tablespaces and archived redo log files must be accessible to RMAN. The transport process occurs in the following steps:

1. RMAN starts an auxiliary instance on the same host as the source database. This instance is used to perform the restore and recovery of the tablespaces.
2. RMAN restores a backup of the source database control file to serve as the auxiliary instance control file.
3. RMAN restores auxiliary set and transportable set data files from the backups of the source database. The auxiliary set includes files that are required for the tablespace transport but which are not part of the transportable tablespace set. It typically includes the SYSTEM and SYSAUX tablespaces, temp files, and data files containing rollback or undo segments.

4. RMAN performs database point-in-time recovery (DBPITR) at the auxiliary instance as of the target time specified for the TRANSPORT TABLESPACE command. When a target time is not specified, the recovery uses all available redo.
5. RMAN opens the auxiliary database with the RESETLOGS options.
6. RMAN places the transportable set tablespaces of the auxiliary instance into read-only mode. It then executes Data Pump Export in transportable tablespace mode to create the export dump file for the transportable set.
7. If the preceding steps are successful, then RMAN shuts down the auxiliary instance and deletes all files created during the operation except for the transportable set files, the Data Pump Export file, and the sample import script.

The following limitations apply to transporting tablespaces:

- The source and the destination databases must use compatible database character sets.
- The destination database cannot contain a tablespace of the same name. If it does, you must rename either the tablespace to be transported or the one in the destination database.
- Objects with underlying objects (such as materialized views) or contained objects (such as partitioned tables) are not transportable unless all of the underlying or contained objects are in the tablespace being transported.
- Transportable tablespaces cannot transport tables with TIMESTAMP WITH TIMEZONE (TSTZ) data across platforms with different time zone file versions.
- Transportable tablespaces cannot transport encrypted tablespaces or tablespaces containing tables with encrypted columns.
- Administrative tablespaces, such as SYSTEM and SYSAUX, cannot be included in a transportable tablespace set.
- Tablespaces that do not use block encryption but that contain tables with encrypted columns cannot be transported.

Transport databases using data files or backup sets

The transportable database feature is essentially an extension of the transportable tablespaces feature that allows Data Pump to handle tablespaces that cannot be transported. When performing a full database export, Data Pump has a new full transportable export option. A full transportable export is performed when the TRANSPORTABLE=ALWAYS parameter is specified along with the FULL parameter. This functionality exports all objects and data required to create a complete copy of the database. Two data movement methods are performed by Data Pump depending on whether the tablespaces are transportable or not:

- **Non-transportable tablespaces** -- Tablespaces like SYSTEM and SYSAUX that cannot be transported have both their metadata and data unloaded into the dump file set, using direct path unload and external tables.
- **Transportable tablespaces** -- For transportable tablespaces, only metadata is unloaded into the dump file set. The contents of the tablespaces are moved when the data files are copied to the target database.

There are several restrictions for performing a full transportable export, including:

- The DATAPUMP_EXP_FULL_DATABASE privilege is required to perform this operation.
- The default tablespace of the user performing the export must not be set to one of the tablespaces being transported.
- If the database being exported contains either encrypted tablespaces or tables with encrypted columns, the ENCRYPTION_PASSWORD parameter must be supplied.
- If there are encrypted tablespaces in the source database, the source and target databases must be on platforms with the same endianness.
- If the source platform and the target platform are of different endianness, then you must convert the data being transported so that it is in the format of the target platform.

- A full transportable export is not restartable.
- All objects with storage that are selected for export must have all of their storage segments either entirely within administrative, non-transportable tablespaces (SYSTEM / SYSAUX) or entirely within user-defined, transportable tablespaces. Storage for a single object cannot straddle the two kinds of tablespaces.

The new functionality can be used to move a non-CDB into a pluggable database (PDB) or to move a PDB into another PDB. Full transportable operations can reduce both the export time and import times required for a full export. When this option is used, table data does not need to be unloaded and reloaded and index structures in user tablespaces do not need to be re-created. The full transportable feature is ideal for moving a database to a new computer system or upgrading to a new release of Oracle.

Transport data across platforms

It is possible to transport tablespaces from an Oracle database on one platform to an Oracle database on a different platform. If the source and destination platforms have the same endian format, it is possible to simply copy the associated files from one platform to the other using operating system commands. The RMAN CONVERT command is required when transporting tablespaces when the endian formats are different between the source and destination platforms. If the entire database is being moved, even if the platforms have the same endian format, any data files with undo information must be converted using RMAN.

Tablespace conversion is performed using the RMAN CONVERT TABLESPACE command on the **source** host only. The command will generate output files in the correct format for the destination platform. The data files in the source database are not altered by the CONVERT command.

The RMAN CONVERT DATAFILE command can be used to convert files on the **destination** host only. Because the data files are not associated with any given tablespace on the destination, individual files must be specified by name in RMAN.

The list of available platforms and their respective endian formats are available from the V$TRANSPORTABLE_TABLESPACE view:

```
SELECT platform_id, platform_name, endian_format
FROM   v$transportable_platform
WHERE  platform_name LIKE '%Linux%';

PLATFORM_ID PLATFORM_NAME                 ENDIAN_FORMAT
----------- ----------------------------- --------------
         10 Linux IA (32-bit)             Little
         11 Linux IA (64-bit)             Little
          9 IBM zSeries Based Linux       Big
         13 Linux x86 64-bit              Little
         18 IBM Power Based Linux         Big
```

Duplicating a Database

Choose a technique for duplicating a database

From an active database, connected to the target and auxiliary instances

Advantages:

- Active duplication can be performed for a database even if backups of it do not exist.
- Requires less disk space on the destination because data is transferred directly from the source database to the destination database.
- RMAN can employ unused block compression while creating backups to reduce the size of backups that are transported over the network.

Disadvantages/Requirements:

- Because active duplication copies mounted or online database files over the network to the auxiliary instance it will generate considerable network traffic during the duplication process.
- The source database must run processes that are used in transferring the files to the auxiliary host. This will negatively affect the performance of the source database and production workload.
- Requires that the target and auxiliary instances use the same password as the source database.
- Requires that a recovery catalog exist.

From backup, connected to the target and auxiliary instances

Advantages:

- Backup files can be transferred to the destination host prior to starting the duplicate operation. This will eliminate the problem of network traffic during the duplication process.
- The performance impact on the source database during the duplication operation is reduced because source database does not need to run processes for transferring files to the auxiliary host.
- The target and auxiliary instances do not need to use the same password as the source database.

Disadvantages/Requirements:

- Requires that backups of for the source database exist.
- Requires more disk space on the destination host if backups are transferred there.
- The backup files on the destination host must have the same file specification as they had on the source host.

From backup, connected to the auxiliary instance, not connected to the target, but with recovery catalog connection

Advantages:

- Backup files can be transferred to the destination host prior to starting the duplicate operation. This will eliminate the problem of network traffic during the duplication process.
- The target and auxiliary instances do not need to use the same password as the source database.
- Useful when network connections from the auxiliary host to the source database are restricted or prone to intermittent disruptions.
- In duplication without a TARGET connection, the source database is unaffected by the duplication.

Disadvantages/Requirements:

- Requires that backups of for the source database exist.
- Requires more disk space on the destination host if backups are transferred there.
- The backup files on the destination host must have the same file specification as they had on the source host.
- Requires that a recovery catalog exist.

From backup, connected to the auxiliary instance, not connected to the target and the recovery catalog

Advantages:

- Backup files can be transferred to the destination host prior to starting the duplicate operation. This will eliminate the problem of network traffic during the duplication process.
- The target and auxiliary instances do not need to use the same password as the source database.
- Useful when network connections from the auxiliary host to the source database are restricted or prone to intermittent disruptions.
- In duplication without a TARGET connection, the source database is unaffected by the duplication.

Disadvantages/Requirements:

- Requires that backups of for the source database exist.
- Requires more disk space on the destination host if backups are transferred there.
- The backup files on the destination host must have the same file specification as they had on the source host.
- Must supply the location of the backups to be used via the BACKUP LOCATION clause.

Duplicate a database with RMAN

The RMAN DUPLICATE command is used to copy all or a subset of the data in a source database. Once created, the duplicate database will function independently from the source database. There are several cases in which it can be useful to create a duplicate database:

- Test backup and recovery procedures
- Test an upgrade to a new release of Oracle Database
- Test the effect of applications on database performance
- Create a standby database
- Generate reports without impacting performance on the source database

When the DUPLICATE command creates a copy of the source database, it can be one of the following:

- **A duplicate database** -- This is a copy of the source database (or a subset of the source database) with a unique DBID. Because it has a unique DBID, the copy is independent of the source and can be registered in the same recovery catalog.
- **A standby database** -- A standby database acts as a backup for the source (or primary) database. It is not assigned a new DBID and the standby is continually updated by applying archived redo log files from the primary database.

If a database is copied using operating system utilities rather than the DUPLICATE command, the DBID of the copy will always be the same as the original database. It is not possible to register the copy in the same recovery catalog with the original unless the DBID is changed with the DBNEWID utility.

RMAN supports two basic types of duplication: active database duplication and backup-based duplication. When backup-based duplication is used, it can be performed with or without either of the following connections:

- Target Database
- Recovery catalog

When performing active database duplication, a connection to both is required.

Create a backup-up based duplicate database

When performing a backup-based recovery, the FROM ACTIVE DATABASE clause of the DUPLICATE command is not specified. Not specifying this clause effectively tells RMAN to perform backup-based duplication. Examples of each of the three types of backup-based duplication follow:

Backup-Based Duplication with a Target Connection

In the following example, RMAN is connected as TARGET to the source database. The DUPLICATE operation recovers the duplicate database to 4 days prior to the current date. All of the data in the copied database will contain the data from the source database as it appeared at that time. The NOFILENAMECHECK option must be specified when the duplicate database files use the same names as the source database files.

```
DUPLICATE TARGET DATABASE TO ocpdup
SPFILE
NOFILENAMECHECK
UNTIL TIME 'SYSDATE-4';
```

Backup-Based Duplication Without a Target Connection

In this example, RMAN does not use a TARGET connection to the source database. The example DUPLICATE command will create a duplicate of the source database ocpdb as it existed on Jun 1st, 2012. Because RMAN is not connected to the source database and no BACKUP LOCATION clause is provided, it must be connected to a recovery catalog in order to obtain the metadata about the backups to be used for the operation.

```
DUPLICATE DATABASE ocpdb DBID 5349873 TO ocpdup
UNTIL TIME "TO_DATE('06/01/2012', 'MM/DD/YYYY')"
SPFILE
NOFILENAMECHECK;
```

Backup-Based Duplication Without a Target or Recovery Catalog Connection

In the following example RMAN does not use a TARGET connection to the source database or a CATALOG connection to a recovery catalog. The BACKUP LOCATION clause specifies the directory '/u01/ocpback'. All of the backup and copies required for the duplication, including a control file backup or copy, must exist in that directory in order for the operation to succeed.

```
DUPLICATE DATABASE TO ocpdup
UNTIL TIME "TO_DATE('02/01/2014 12:00:00', 'MM/DD/YYYY HH24:MI:SS')"
SPFILE
BACKUP LOCATION '/u01/ocpback'
NOFILENAMECHECK;
```

Duplicate a database based on a running instance

There are numerous different options when duplicating a database. The example shown below makes use of the most basic procedure to duplicate a database. It assumes that the entire database is being duplicated to a remote host and that the filenames will be the same as the source database files. When the filenames are not being changed, the NOFILENAMECHECK option must be specified on the DUPLICATE command. When duplicating a database to the same host as the source database, the filenames must be changed and NOFILENAMECHECK must not be specified. The following example duplicates a database to a remote host with the same directory structure follow:

```
DUPLICATE TARGET DATABASE TO ocpdup
FROM ACTIVE DATABASE
PASSWORD FILE
SPFILE
NOFILENAMECHECK;
```

The PASSWORD FILE option in the example above specifies that RMAN should copy the password file to the destination host. As part of the above operation, RMAN will perform the following actions:

1. Copy the server parameter file to the destination host.
2. Restart the auxiliary instance with the server parameter file.
3. Copy all necessary database files and archived redo logs over the network to the destination host.
4. Recover the database.
5. Open the database with the RESETLOGS option to create the online redo log.

Monitoring and Tuning of RMAN Operations

Tune RMAN performance

Interpret RMAN error stacks

RMAN reports errors as they occur. If RMAN is unable to perform failover to another channel to complete a particular job step, it will report a summary of the errors after all job sets complete. It is possible to determine whether RMAN encountered an error by searching the RMAN output for the string RMAN-00569. This is message number for the error stack banner which will precede all RMAN errors. If the output does not contain RMAN-00569, there are no errors. Typically, the following types of error codes occur in RMAN message stacks:

- Errors prefixed with RMAN-
- Errors prefixed with ORA-
- Errors preceded by the line Additional information:

When interpreting RMAN Error Stacks the following tips and suggestions can assist:

- The messages should be read from the bottom up, because this is the order in which RMAN issues the messages. The lowest one or two errors in the stack are generally the most informative.
- Look for the RMAN-03002 or RMAN-03009 message immediately following the error banner. These messages indicate which command failed.
- Refer to Oracle Database Error Messages for further information about the messages.

The following is an example of an RMAN error stack. An attempt was made to backup the OCP_USERS tablespace and the following message was generated:

```
Starting backup at 24-MAY-15
using channel ORA_DISK_1
RMAN-00571:
===========================================================
RMAN-00569: =============== ERROR MESSAGE STACK FOLLOWS
===============
RMAN-00571:
===========================================================
RMAN-03002: failure of backup command at 05/24/2015 12:31:19
RMAN-20202: tablespace not found in the recovery catalog
RMAN-06019: could not translate tablespace name "OPC_USERS"
```

The RMAN-03002 error indicates that the BACKUP command failed. Based on the last two messages in the stack, it is obvious that the problem was caused by the OCP_USERS tablespace being misspelled in the backup command.

Diagnose performance bottlenecks

It is possible to use the V$BACKUP_SYNC_IO and V$BACKUP_ASYNC_IO views to locate the source of backup or restore bottlenecks.

- **V$BACKUP_SYNC_IO** -- Contains rows when the I/O is synchronous to the process (or thread on some platforms) performing the backup.
- **V$BACKUP_ASYNC_IO** -- Contains rows when the I/O is asynchronous. Asynchronous I/O is obtained either with I/O processes or because it is supported by the underlying operating system.

Despite the fact that these are dynamic performance views, the results of a backup or restore job remain in memory until the database instance shuts down. This allows the views to be queried even after the backup or restore job has completed. When a backup or restore operation is going to or coming from a tape, it is possible to determine whether the tape is streaming as follows:

1. Start SQL*Plus and connect to the target database.
2. Query the EFFECTIVE_BYTES_PER_SECOND column in the V$BACKUP_SYNC_IO or V$BACKUP_ASYNC_IO view.

If the value of EFFECTIVE_BYTES_PER_SECOND is less than the raw capacity of the hardware, then the tape is not streaming. When the value is greater than the raw capacity of the hardware, the tape may be streaming. The effects of compression can cause the EFFECTIVE_BYTES_PER_SECOND value to be greater than the speed of actual I/O.

Identifying specific bottlenecks with synchronous I/O is difficult because all synchronous I/O acts a bottleneck to the process. The only metric for tuning synchronous I/O is comparing the rate (in bytes per second) with the device's maximum throughput rate. When the rate is lower than the maximum specified for the device specifies, it might be worthwhile to tune tuning this aspect of the backup and restore process. The steps to determine the rate of synchronous I/O are:

1. Start SQL*Plus and connect to the target database.
2. Query the DISCRETE_BYTES_PER_SECOND column in the V$BACKUP_SYNC_IO view to display the I/O rate.

If there is data in V$BACKUP_SYNC_IO, then asynchronous I/O is not enabled or disk I/O slaves are not being used.

When working with asynchronous I/O, there are two types of waits:

- **Long waits** -- This is the number of times a backup or restore process told the operating system to wait until an I/O was complete.

- **Short waits** -- This is the number of times the backup or restore process made an operating system call to poll for I/O completion in a nonblocking mode.

The steps to determine the rate of asynchronous I/O are:

1. Start SQL*Plus and connect to the target database.
2. Query the LONG_WAITS and IO_COUNT columns in the V$BACKUP_SYNC_IO view to display the I/O rate.

One way to identify an asynchronous I/O bottleneck is to locate the data file that has the largest ratio for LONG_WAITS divided by IO_COUNT. The following query is an example of this:

```
SELECT long_waits / io_count, filename
FROM   v$backup_async_io
WHERE  long_waits / io_count > 0
ORDER BY long_waits / io_count DESC;
```

Tune RMAN backup performance

There are a number of different factors involved in RMAN performance. This section covers many different ways of increasing RMAN performance, reducing the load it places on the database, or both.

RATE

The RMAN commands ALLOCATE and CONFIGURE CHANNEL both have a RATE parameter. This is used to specify the bytes per second that are read on a channel. It is intended to set an upper limit for bytes read in order to prevent RMAN from consuming excessive disk bandwidth. This ensures that there is disk bandwidth available for other database operations. If the backup is not streaming to tape, the RATE parameter should not be set.

Large Pool

RMAN is one of several users of the large pool. The total size of the pool must be sufficient for all the processes that use it. This is especially true if the DBWR_IO_SLAVES parameter has been set. The value of the LARGE_POOL_SIZE initialization parameter should be set or increased if the database reports an error in the alert log stating that there is insufficient memory to start I/O slaves. The error message will be similar to the following:

```
ksfqxcre: failure to allocate shared memory means sync I/O will be
used whenever async I/O to file not supported natively
```

To set the large pool size:

1. Start SQL*Plus and connect to the target database.
2. Set the LARGE_POOL_SIZE initialization parameter in the target database.
3. The ALTER SYSTEM SET statement can be used to set the parameter dynamically.
4. ALTER SYSTEM SET LARGE_POOL_SIZE = 512M scope=both;
5. Restart the RMAN backup.

Multiplexing

When performing an incremental backup, RMAN will only back up blocks that have changed since a previous backup that is part of the same strategy. If block change tracking is not enabled, RMAN must scan the entire data file for changed blocks. The changed blocks are written to output buffers as RMAN finds them. If relatively few blocks changed while RMAN is making an SBT backup, the output buffers may not fill fast enough to keep the tape drive streaming. In these cases, it is possible to improve backup performance by adjusting the level of multiplexing. This is the number of input files that are simultaneously read and written to the same RMAN backup piece. The level of multiplexing is determined by the smaller of the number of input files placed in each backup set and the MAXOPENFILES setting on the channel.

Tuning the Copy and Write Phases

There are several options for tuning the Copy and Write phases depending on the circumstances. Some alternatives for improving this are:

- If the performance issue is with a full backup, consider using incremental backups. Incremental level 1 backups write only the changed blocks from data files to tape. If there is a bottleneck when writing to tape, this will reduce the impact on the overall backup strategy.
- For backups that use the basic compression algorithm, consider using the Advanced Compression Option.
- On a database host with multiple CPUs and a backup using binary compression, try increasing the number of channels.
- For an encrypted backup, change the encryption to AES128, which is the least CPU-intensive algorithm.
- If RMAN is backing up files to ASM, then increase the number of channels up to a maximum of 16.

You can use the DURATION parameter of the BACKUP command to limit the amount of time a given backup job is given to run. To specify a backup duration:

```
BACKUP
DURATION 4:00
TABLESPACE users;
```

The above command will generate an error if the backup does not complete inside the window. If the keyword PARTIAL is specified, RMAN does not report an error but rather displays a message showing which files are not backed up. If the BACKUP command is part of a RUN block, then the remaining commands in the RUN block continue to execute.

Specifying FILESPERSET of 1 will save each file as its own backup set. If the window closes before the backup is complete, only the current set (one file) is lost. The following example prevents RMAN from issuing an error and minimizes lost work when a backup partially completes:

```
BACKUP
DURATION 4:00 PARTIAL
TABLESPACE users
FILESPERSET 1;
```

Minimizing Backup Load and Duration

When using DURATION you can run the backup with the maximum possible performance, or run as slowly as possible while still finishing within the allotted time, to minimize the performance impact of backup tasks. To maximize performance, use the MINIMIZE TIME option with DURATION.

```
BACKUP
DURATION 4:00 PARTIAL
MINIMIZE TIME
DATABASE
FILESPERSET 1;
```

When MINIMIZE LOAD is specified, RMAN monitors the progress of the running backup, and periodically estimates how long the backup will take to complete at its present rate. If RMAN estimates that the backup will finish before the end of the backup window, then it slows down the rate of backup so that the full available duration is used. This reduces the overhead on the database associated with the backup. To extend the backup to use the full time available, use the MINIMIZE LOAD option:

```
BACKUP
DURATION 4:00 PARTIAL
MINIMIZE LOAD
DATABASE
FILESPERSET 1;
```

When an RMAN channel accesses a disk for read or write operations, the I/O is either synchronous or asynchronous. When performing synchronous I/O, a server process can perform only one task at a time. When using asynchronous I/O, a server process can begin an I/O operation and then perform some other task while waiting for the I/O to complete. It is also possible to start additional I/O operations without having to wait for the first to complete. When reading from an ASM disk group, you should use asynchronous disk I/O if possible.

Disk I/O Slaves

Many operating systems support asynchronous I/O natively. If an operating system does not support native asynchronous I/O, the database can use special I/O slave processes to simulate it. The availability of disk I/O slaves is controlled by setting the DBWR_IO_SLAVES initialization parameter. By default, the value is 0 and I/O server processes are not used. Set DBWR_IO_SLAVES to enable RMAN to perform asynchronous I/O if and only if your disk does not support asynchronous I/O natively. Any nonzero value for DBWR_IO_SLAVES causes a fixed number of disk I/O slaves to be used for backup and restore, which simulates asynchronous I/O. To enable disk I/O slaves:

1. Start SQL*Plus and connect to the target database.
2. Shut down the database.
3. Set DBWR_IO_SLAVES initialization parameter to a nonzero value.
4. Restart the database.

Tape I/O Slaves

The initialization parameter BACKUP_TAPE_IO_SLAVES specifies whether or not RMAN uses slave processes. Tape devices can only be accessed by a single process at one time, so RMAN uses only the number of slaves necessary for the number of tape devices. If set to true, RMAN will allocate tape buffers from the SGA. When the LARGE_POOL_SIZE initialization parameter is also set, then RMAN allocates buffers from the large pool. When BACKUP_TAPE_IO_SLAVES is set to false, RMAN allocates tape buffers from the PGA. When making use of I/O slaves, set the LARGE_POOL_SIZE initialization parameter to dedicate space for these large memory allocations. This prevents RMAN I/O buffers from competing with the library cache for SGA memory.

Oracle Database 12c: Managing Multitenant Architecture

Multitenant Container and Pluggable Database Architecture

Describe the multitenant architecture

Oracle 12c introduced a radical new architecture with the Multitenant option. The new architecture allows for Oracle to be provisioned as a 'Container' database (CDB) that can host multiple 'Pluggable' databases (PDBs) -- each of which can be added and removed from the CDB. Existing legacy Oracle databases can be adapted to become pluggable databases. The new PDBs in turn can continue to be accessed by other tiers without having to make changes to legacy applications.

There are a number of advantages to the Multitenant architecture, including:

- **Database Consolidation** -- Multiple pluggable databases can be stored in a single container database. When in a CDB, they share a single set of background processes, server and system memory while still maintaining complete separation of the data in each PDB. There is no added maintenance overhead or mingling of data as is the case with Virtual Private Databases. This makes it possible to store many more PDBs on a given hardware platform than individual Oracle databases using the legacy architecture.
- **Reduced Costs** -- Consolidating multiple databases can dramatically reduce the costs associated with hardware. In addition, a container database with a dozen PDBs requires considerably less maintenance than twelve individual databases. The result requires fewer personnel to maintain.
- **Rapid Implementation** -- Pluggable databases make it very easy to migrate or implement data and code. It requires very little time to plug a PDB into a CDB, unplug it, and then plug the PDB into a different CDB.

- **Simplified Management** -- With multiple PDBs in a single container database, it is simpler for database administrators to monitor and manage the physical database. There is only a single set of database files and one instance to maintain. This simplifies both backup strategies and disaster recovery scenarios.
- **Separation of administrative duties** -- Multitenant user accounts are either common, which allows them to connect to any container on which they have privileges, or local, and can only connect to a single PDB. DBA duties in turn can be split between CDB-level and PDB level. CDB administrators use a common account to manage the CDB. PDB administrators use local accounts to manage individual PDBs. Privileges exist only in the container for which they are granted. A local user on one PDB does not have privileges on other PDBs within the same CDB.
- **Simplified Tuning** -- Monitoring and tuning one database is much easier than monitoring and tuning a dozen databases.
- **Simplified Patching** -- Patching/upgrading a single database is much easier than doing so for a dozen databases.

The multitenant architecture is what allows an Oracle database to act as a container database that includes zero, one, or many PDBs. A container is a collection of schemas, objects, and related structures stored in a multitenant container database. A container is either a PDB or the root container (also called the root). Each PDB appears logically to an application as a separate database. Within a CDB, each PDB container must have a unique ID and name. PDBs isolate data and operations so that from the perspective of a user or application accessing it through Oracle Net, each PDB appears as if it were a traditional database.

Every container database has the following containers:

- **One root** -- The root container stores Oracle-supplied metadata (such as the source code for Oracle-supplied PL/SQL packages) and common users. A common user is a database user known in every container. The root container is named CDB$ROOT. All PDBs belong to the root. User data should never be stored in the root and the system-supplied schemas should never be altered. It is possible, however, to create common users and roles for database administration.

- **One seed PDB** -- The seed PDB is a system-supplied template that can be used to create new PDBs. The seed PDB is named PDB$SEED. You cannot add or modify objects in PDB$SEED.
- **Zero or more user-created PDBs** -- User-created PDBs are the entities that contain the data and code required for a specific set of features. No PDBs exist at the time the CDB is initially created. PDBs are added to the container database as needed. PDBs must be uniquely named within a CDB, and follow the same naming rules as service names. Moreover, because a PDB has a service with its own name, a PDB name must be unique across all CDBs whose services are exposed through a specific listener.

Explain pluggable database provisioning

Part of Enterprise Manager Cloud Control's Provisioning capability includes the ability to manipulate pluggable databases. EM Cloud Control enables administrators to manage the entire PDB lifecycle. This includes provisioning CDBs, provisioning PDBs (from the seed or from an unplugged PDB), cloning existing PDBs, migrating non-CDBs as PDBs, and unplugging PDBs. From EM Cloud control, it is possible to provision PDBs in several different ways:

- Create a new PDB within a CDB
- Cloning an existing PDB
- Migrating existing non-CDBs to a CDB as PDBs
- Plugging an unplugged PDB into a CDB

The first two of the above operations create a new pluggable database and attach it to an existing Container Database. The second two simply attach an existing database to a CDB. When a PDB becomes part of a CDB, it runs under the umbrella of the CDB, sharing the instance, undo tablespace and various other functionality that will be described in the following topics.

Creating Multitenant Container Databases and Pluggable Databases

Configure and create a CDB

The steps involved in creating a container database are very much like those required to create a standard Oracle database. Prior to creating the CDB, you must take into account what the database will be used for and plan accordingly. Some of the recommended pre-creation actions include:

- Plan the tables and indexes for the pluggable databases (PDBs) that will be contained in the CDB and estimate the amount of space they will require.
- Plan the layout of the underlying operating system files for the CDB.
- Plan for the number of background processes that the CDB will require.
- Determine the global database name for the CDB to be set by the DB_NAME and DB_DOMAIN initialization parameters.
- Develop a backup and recovery strategy to protect the CDB from failure.
- Select an appropriate character set.
- Determine the appropriate initial size for the SYSAUX tablespace.

Before a new CDB can be created, the following prerequisites must be met:

- Oracle 12c must be installed with the database compatibility level to at least 12.0.0.
- Sufficient memory must be available to start the Oracle Database instance.
- Sufficient disk storage space must be available for the planned PDBs on the computer that runs Oracle Database.

The container database creation prepares several operating system files to work together as a CDB. A CDB can be created either during or after Oracle Database software installation. A CDB can be created either with the Database Configuration Assistant (DBCA) or with the CREATE DATABASE SQL statement. Oracle strongly recommends using the Database Configuration Assistant (DBCA) method. DBCA is a much easier method for doing so and the CDB is ready to use as soon as DBCA completes.

The Database Configuration Assistant can be launched by the Oracle Universal Installer or launched as a standalone tool at any time after Oracle Database installation. It is possible to create a CDB in interactive mode or noninteractive/silent mode. The interactive mode provides a graphical interface and guided workflow for the CDB creation process. Noninteractive mode enables you to script the creation of the CDB. Once the CDB has been created, DBCA can be used to plug new PDBs into it or unplug existing ones.

If you decide to use the CREATE DATABASE statement to create a CDB, there are additional actions that must be completed before the CDB will be operational. Namely, the standard PL/SQL packages must be installed and required views created against the data dictionary tables. The catcdb.sql script must be executed to perform these actions.

Create a PDB using different methods

Prior to creating a PDB, several prerequisites must be met:

- The CDB must exist.
- The CDB must be in read/write mode.
- The current user must be a common user whose current container is the root.
- The current user must have the CREATE PLUGGABLE DATABASE system privilege.
- A PDB name must be selected that is unique to the CDB it will be plugged into and all the CDBs whose instances are reached through a specific listener.

- PDBs created in an Oracle Data Guard configuration with a physical standby database, have additional requirements. Reference the Oracle Data Guard Concepts and Administration manual for more information.

There are four different methods for creating a pluggable database (PDB) in a multitenant container database (CDB):

- **Using the seed** -- The files associated with the seed are copied to a new location and associated with the new PDB.
- **Cloning an existing PDB** -- An existing PDB can be cloned and plugged into the CDB. The PDB to be used as the source can either be in the local CDB or in a remote CDB. All of the files associated with the source PDB are copied to a new location and associated with the new PDB.
- **Plugging in an unplugged PDB** -- The XML metadata file that describes an unplugged PDB plus its associated files are plugged into the CDB.
- **Converting a non-CDB** -- The DBMS_PDB package can create an unplugged PDB from an Oracle Database 12c non-CDB. The newly-created PDB can then be plugged into a CDB.

All four techniques make use of the CREATE PLUGGABLE DATABASE statement at some point. This statement is used for both copying a database and for plugging a PDB in to a CDB as required. The statement has optional clauses that can be used to set several aspects of the PDB:

- **Storage** – The STORAGE clause specifies the amount of storage that can be used by all tablespaces that belong to the PDB and the amount of storage in the default temporary tablespace shared by all PDBs that can be used by sessions connected to the PDB. If STORAGE UNLIMITED is set, or if there is no STORAGE clause, the PDB has no storage limits.
- **File Locations** -- There are three clauses that affect the file names used for a PDB. The PATH_PREFIX clause can be used to ensure that a PDB's files reside in a specific directory and its subdirectories when relative paths are used for directory objects

and certain initialization parameters. The FILE_NAME_CONVERT clause specifies the names of the PDB's files after the PDB is plugged into the CDB. The SOURCE_FILE_NAME_CONVERT clause specifies the names of a PDB's files before the PDB is plugged into the CDB.

- **Temp File Reuse** -- The TEMPFILE REUSE clause specifies that an existing temp file in the target location is reused if one exists. If this clause is specified, and there is no temp file in the target location, Oracle will create a new temp file. If the clause is not specified, Oracle will attempt to create a new temp file for the PDB. If a file exists with the same name as the new temp file in the target location, an error will be generated, and the PDB creation will fail.

Creating a PDB Using the Seed

The CREATE PLUGGABLE DATABASE statement can be used to create a PDB in a CDB using the files of the seed. When creating a new PDB from the seed, a PDB administrator must be specified in the CREATE PLUGGABLE DATABASE statement. The new database will be created with two tablespaces: SYSTEM and SYSAUX. The administrator is created as a local user in the PDB and granted the PDB_DBA role. To create a PDB from the seed:

- In SQL*Plus, ensure that the current container is the root.
- Run the CREATE PLUGGABLE DATABASE statement, and specify a local administrator for the PDB. Specify other clauses when they are required.
- Open the new PDB in read/write mode that that Oracle can complete the integration of the new PDB into the CDB.
- Back up the PDB.

An example of this method (with none of the optional clauses) is:

```
CREATE PLUGGABLE DATABASE ocp_pdb ADMIN USER ocp_adm IDENTIFIED BY
password;
```

Cloning a PDB

The CREATE PLUGGABLE DATABASE statement can be used to clone a PDB. When cloning an existing PDB, the FROM clause will specify the source PDB to be cloned. The source PDB can be in the local CDB or in a remote CDB. In order to clone a PDB, the current user must have the CREATE PLUGGABLE DATABASE system privilege in both the root and the source PDB and the source PDB must be open in read-only mode. To clone a PDB:

- In SQL*Plus, ensure that the current container is the root.
- Run the CREATE PLUGGABLE DATABASE statement, and specify the source PDB in the FROM clause. Specify other clauses when they are required.
- Open the new PDB in read/write mode.
- Back up the PDB.

An example of the syntax for cloning a PDB is:

```
CREATE PLUGGABLE DATABASE pdb2 FROM pdb1
PATH_PREFIX = '/u02/oracle/pdb2'
FILE_NAME_CONVERT = ('/u01/oracle/pdb1/', '/u02/oracle/pdb2/');
```

Plugging an Unplugged PDB into a CDB

This technique uses the XML metadata file of an existing PDB along with its associated files to plug it into the CDB. The USING clause of the CREATE PLUGGABLE DATABASE statement specifies the XML metadata file. The XML file in turn contains the locations of the PDB's files. To plug in an unplugged PDB:

- In SQL*Plus, ensure that the current container is the root.
- (Optional) Run the DBMS_PDB.CHECK_PLUG_COMPATIBILITY function to determine whether the unplugged PDB is compatible with the CDB.

- Run the CREATE PLUGGABLE DATABASE statement, and specify the XML file in the USING clause. Specify other clauses when they are required.
- Open the new PDB in read/write mode.
- Back up the PDB.

An example of the syntax for plugging in an unplugged PDB is:

```
CREATE PLUGGABLE DATABASE ocp_pdb USING '/u01/usr/ocp_pdb.xml'
NOCOPY TEMPFILE REUSE;
```

Creating a PDB Using a Non-CDB

It is possible to move a non-CDB into a PDB via three different methods:

- **DBMS_PDB** -- The DBMS_PDB package can be used to generate an XML metadata file. This file describes the database files of the non-CDB . It can then be plugged into a CDB using the XML file as described above. In order to use this technique, the non-CDB must be from an Oracle 12c Database. Older databases must be upgraded to Oracle Database 12c in order to use this technique.
- **Oracle Data Pump** -- With this method, Oracle Data Pump is used to export the data from the non-CDB database so that it can then be imported into a PDB.
- **Goldengate replication** -- In this method data is replicated from the non-CDB to a PDB. When the PDB catches up with the non-CDB, you fail over to the PDB.

Unplug and drop a PDB

Unplugging a PDB disassociates it from the CDB. This might be done in order to move the PDB to a different CDB or because there is no longer a need for the PDB to be available. When a PDB is unplugged, the ALTER PLUGGABLE DATABASE statement will specify an XML file to contain metadata about the PDB after it is unplugged. The XML file will be created by the operation and will contain information that will allow a CREATE PLUGGABLE DATABASE statement on a target CDB to plug in the PDB.

The unplug operation makes some changes in the PDB's data files, including recording the PDB was successfully unplugged. An unplugged PDB is still part of the CDB, and will be included in an RMAN backup of the entire CDB. To completely remove the PDB from the CDB, it must be dropped. The only operation supported on an unplugged PDB is to drop it. An unplugged PDB cannot be plugged back into the same database unless it is dropped. In order to unplug a PDB, the following prerequisites must be met:

- The user must be connected to the root with the SYSDBA or SYSOPER administrative privilege.
- The PDB must have been opened at least once.
- The PDB must be closed.

To unplug a PDB:

1. In SQL*Plus, connect to the root as SYSDBA or SYSOPER.
2. Run the ALTER PLUGGABLE DATABASE statement with the UNPLUG INTO clause, and specify the PDB to unplug and the name and location of the PDB's XML metadata file. The following statement unplugs the PDB ocp_pdb and creates the ocp_pdb.xml metadata file in the /oracle/data/ directory:

```
ALTER PLUGGABLE DATABASE ocp_pdb
  UNPLUG INTO '/oracle/data/ocp_pdb.xml';
```

The DROP PLUGGABLE DATABASE statement is used to drop a PDB. A PDB might be dropped in order to move it to another CDB or when it is no longer needed. When a PDB is dropped, the control file of the CDB is modified to eliminate all references to it. And archived redo log files and backups that are associated with the PDB are not removed by the DROP statement. Oracle Recovery Manager (RMAN) can be used to remove them. When a PDB is dropped, it is possible to either keep or delete the data files associated with it by using one of the following clauses:

- **KEEP DATAFILES** -- This is the default, and retains the data files. The PDB's temp file is removed even when KEEP DATAFILES is specified because it is no longer needed.
- **INCLUDING DATAFILES** -- This option removes the data files from disk. For a PDB that was created with the SNAPSHOT COPY clause, INCLUDING DATAFILES must be specified when dropping the PDB.

In order to drop a PDB, the following prerequisites must be met:

- The PDB must be in mounted mode, or it must be unplugged.
- The user must be connected to the root with the SYSDBA or SYSOPER administrative privilege.

To drop a PDB:

1. In SQL*Plus, connect to the root as SYSDBA or SYSOPER.
2. Run the DROP PLUGGABLE DATABASE statement and specify the PDB to drop.

```
DROP PLUGGABLE DATABASE ocpdb
INCLUDING DATAFILES;
```

Migrate a non-CDB to a PDB database

It is possible to move a non-CDB into a PDB via three different methods:

- **DBMS_PDB** -- The DBMS_PDB package can be used to generate an XML metadata file. This file describes the database files of the non-CDB. It can then be plugged into a CDB using the XML file as described above. In order to use this technique, the non-CDB must be from an Oracle 12c Database. Older databases must be upgraded to Oracle Database 12c in order to use this technique.

- **Oracle Data Pump** -- With this method, Oracle Data Pump is used to export the data from the non-CDB database so that it can then be imported into a PDB.
- **Goldengate replication** -- In this method data is replicated from the non-CDB to a PDB. When the PDB catches up with the non-CDB, you fail over to the PDB.

This section will deal with using the DBMS_PDB.DESCRIBE procedure of the DBMS_PDB package. Oracle Data Pump is discussed in a later section and GoldenGate is outside the scope of this exam.

To move a non-CDB into a PDB using the DBMS_PDB package, the CDB must be in a transactionally-consistent state. In addition, it must be placed in read-only mode. Once the non-CDB is read-only, connect to the database, and execute the DBMS_PDB.DESCRIBE procedure. This procedure will construct an XML file that describes the non-CDB. The following example will generate an XML file named ocp_db.xml in the /u01/oracle directory:

```
BEGIN
DBMS_PDB.DESCRIBE(
  pdb_descr_file => '/u01/oracle/ocp_db.xml');
END;
/
```

Once the procedure has completed and the XML file has been created, the XML file and the non-CDB's database files can be plugged into a CDB. Shut down the non-CDB and then issue the CREATE PLUGGABLE DATABASE statement with the appropriate clauses, for example:

```
CREATE PLUGGABLE DATABASE ncdb USING '/u01/oracle/ocp_db.xml'
COPY
FILE_NAME_CONVERT = ('/u01/oracle/dbs/', '/u02/oracle/ocp_db/');
```

Before opening the new PDB for the first time, you must run the ORACLE_HOME/rdbms/admin/noncdb_to_pdb.sql script. This script is only required when converting non-CDB databases into a PDB.

```
@$ORACLE_HOME/rdbms/admin/noncdb_to_pdb.sql
```

After running the script, the new PDB must be opened in read/write mode for Oracle Database to complete the integration of the new PDB into the CDB. An error is returned if you attempt o open the PDB in read-only mode. Once the database has been opened in read-write mode, you should immediately take a backup of the new PDB.

Managing a CDB and PDBs

Establish connections to CDB/PDB

Client applications connecting to a CDB can access the root or a PDB through database services. Database services have an optional PDB property. At the time each new PDB is created, a new default service with the same name as the PDB will be created automatically. When Oracle Net Services is configured properly, it is possible to use the service name to access the PDB using the easy connect syntax or the net service name from the tnsnames.ora file. When a connection is submitted using a service with a non-null PDB property, the user name for the session is resolved in the context of the specified PDB. If no service is specified or a service name with a NULL PDB property is used, the user name will be resolved in the context of the root.

If two or more CDBs on the same computer system use the same listener and they contain two or more PDBs with the same service name, using that service name will connect randomly to one of the PDBs using it. All service names for PDBs should be unique on a given system, or each CDB should use a separate listener.

It is possible to connect to a container by using the SQL*Plus CONNECT command. Alternately, it is possible to switch into a container with an ALTER SESSION SET CONTAINER SQL statement. The CONNECT command can be used to connect either to the root or to a PDB in a CDB. Any of the following techniques are valid for connecting to the root using the SQL*Plus CONNECT command:

- Local connection
- Local connection with operating system authentication
- Database connection using easy connect
- Database connection using a net service name
- Remote database connection using external authentication

In order for a user to connect to the root, they must be a common user and that user must have been granted CREATE SESSION privilege in the root. To connect to the root using the SQL*Plus CONNECT command, you must start SQL*Plus with the /NOLOG argument:

```
sqlplus /nolog
```

Once in SQL*Plus, you can connect to the root by various methods:

- Connecting with a Local Connection
  ```
  connect username/password
  ```

- Connecting with Operating System Authentication
  ```
  connect / as sysdba
  ```

- Connecting with a Net Service Name
  ```
  connect username/password@ocp_db
  ```

Either of the following techniques can be used to connect to a PDB with the SQL*Plus CONNECT command:

- Database connection using easy connect
- Database connection using a net service name

In order to connect to a PDB, a user must be a common user of the CDB with CREATE SESSION granted either commonly or locally in the PDB, or a local user in the PDB with CREATE SESSION granted. Only a user with SYSDBA, SYSOPER, SYSBACKUP, or SYSDG privilege can connect to a PDB that is in mounted mode. To connect to a PDB using the SQL*Plus CONNECT command, you must start SQL*Plus with the /NOLOG argument:

```
sqlplus /nolog
```

The following command connects to the candidate local user in the ocp_db PDB:

```
CONNECT candidate@ocp_db
```

When a session is connected to a container as a common user, the following statement can be used to switch to a different container:

```
ALTER SESSION SET CONTAINER = container_name
```

The container_name, can be any one of the following:

- CDB$ROOT to switch to the root
- PDB$SEED to switch to the seed
- A PDB name to switch to the PDB

Start up and shut down a CDB and open and close PDBs

Unless being operated in a Real Application Clusters environment, a CDB runs with a single instance. The startup process for a CDB instance is same as that for non-CDB databases. STARTUP NOMOUNT, STARTUP MOUNT, and STARTUP OPEN all function in a CDB and have the effect on the Container Database that they would on a non-CDB. However, the status of the PDBs within the CDB is not always the same. You need to be connected to the root of the CDB with SYSDBA privileges in order to start the instance. Once the instance has been started, you may use the V$PDBS view to determine the status of PDBs.

- **NOMOUNT** -- When the CDB is in NOMOUNT status, the instance is started, but the PDBs have no status. Querying the V$PDBS view will return no rows.

- **MOUNT** -- When the CDB is in MOUNT status, the control files for the instance will be opened. The Root and all of the PDBs will be in a status of MOUNTED.
- **OPEN** -- When the CDB is initially set to OPN, the root will be opened. The SEEB PDB will be opened in read-only mode. All other PDBs in the CDB will still be in MOUNTED status.

Once the CDB is opened, it is possible to open the PDBs individually or all at once:

```
ALTER PLUGGABLE DATABASE ocp_db OPEN;
ALTER PLUGGABLE DATABASE ALL OPEN;
```

A CDB instance is shut down in the same fashion that a non-CDB instance is. To shut the instance down, the following requirements must be met:

- It must be mounted or open
- The current user must be a common user with SYSDBA, SYSOPER, SYSBACKUP, or SYSDG administrative privilege
- The current container must be the root.

The open mode of a PDB can be altered using the ALTER PLUGGABLE DATABASE SQL statement or the SQL*Plus STARTUP command. The possible modes for PDBs are:

- **OPEN READ WRITE** -- This mode allows queries and user transactions to proceed and allows users to generate redo logs.
- **OPEN READ ONLY** -- This mode allows queries but does not allow user changes.
- **OPEN MIGRATE** -- This mode allows you to run database upgrade scripts on the PDB. A PDB is in this mode after an ALTER DATABASE OPEN UPGRADE is run.
- **MOUNTED** -- A PDB is in mounted mode behaves like a non-CDB in mounted mode. No changes are allowed to objects and it is accessible only to database administrators.

When the current container is the root, an ALTER PLUGGABLE DATABASE statement with a pdb_change_state clause modifies the open mode of the specified PDBs. When a PDB is opened using the ALTER PLUGGABLE DATABASE OPEN statement, READ WRITE is the default unless the PDB belongs to a CDB that is used as a physical standby database, in which case READ ONLY is the default. The PDBs to be modified by the ALTER statement can be specified in the following ways:

- List one or more PDBs separated by commas.
- Specify ALL to modify all of the PDBs.
- Specify ALL EXCEPT to modify all of the PDBs, except for the PDBs listed.

Some examples of this statement are:

```
ALTER PLUGGABLE DATABASE ocp_db, test_db OPEN READ WRITE;

ALTER PLUGGABLE DATABASE ocp_db OPEN READ ONLY RESTRICTED;

ALTER PLUGGABLE DATABASE ALL OPEN READ WRITE;
```

When the current container is the root it is also possible to use the STARTUP PLUGGABLE DATABASE command to open a single PDB. The STARTUP PLUGGABLE DATABASE statement has the following options:

- **FORCE** -- Closes an open PDB before re-opening it in read/write mode.
- **RESTRICT** -- Enables only users with the RESTRICTED SESSION system privilege in the PDB to access the PDB.
- **OPEN** -- Opens the PDB in either read/write mode or read-only mode. You can specify OPEN READ WRITE or OPEN READ ONLY. When no option is specified, READ WRITE is the default.

Some examples of this statement are:

```
STARTUP PLUGGABLE DATABASE ocp_db OPEN

STARTUP PLUGGABLE DATABASE ocp_db RESTRICT
```

```
STARTUP PLUGGABLE DATABASE ocp_db OPEN READ ONLY

STARTUP PLUGGABLE DATABASE ocp_db FORCE
```

The ALTER PLUGGABLE DATABASE can also be used to close one or more PDBs. To close a PDB, connect to the root as SYSOPER or SYSDBA and issue an ALTER PLUGGABLE DATABASE CLOSE statement, specifying the PDB or PDBs to be closed. If the command is issued with the IMMEDIATE keyword, transactions in the selected PDBs are rolled back and the sessions disconnected. If the IMMEDIATE keyword is omitted, the statement hangs until all sessions have disconnected from the PDB. All of the data files of the PDB will be closed and it will be inaccessible to users. When connected to PDB, issuing a SHUTDOWN IMMEDIATE is equivalent to ALTER PLUGGABLE DATABASE CLOSE.

Some examples of this statement are:

```
ALTER PLUGGABLE DATABASE ocp_db, test_db CLOSE;

ALTER PLUGGABLE DATABASE ALL CLOSE;

ALTER PLUGGABLE DATABASE ALL EXCEPT testdb CLOSE IMMEDIATE;
```

Evaluate the impact of parameter value changes

A CDB will contain only a single SPFILE no matter how many PDBs it contains. Any initialization parameters specified at the root level apply to the root and will be the default value for any PDBs it contains. Many (but not all) initialization parameters can also be set at the PDB level. The parameters that are modifiable for PDBs can be located with the following query:

```
SELECT name
FROM   v$system_parameter
WHERE  ispdb_modifiable = 'TRUE'
ORDER BY name;
```

Any of the initialization parameters listed by this query that are not set independently for a PDB will be inherited from the parameter value set at the root. Values from the list can be set at the PDB level with the ALTER SYSTEM command. When the SCOPE is set to SPFILE or BOTH, the values will be retained across PDB close/open and across bouncing the CDB instance. Parameters set at this level will also travel with clone and unplug/plug operations. Any initialization parameters that do not show up in the above query can be set for the root only.

It is possible to use the ALTER SYSTEM statement to dynamically alter a PDB. Not all possible statements can be run from a PDB. Any statements that affect the entire CDB must be run by a common user in the root. When the current container is a PDB, a user with the proper privileges can execute the following ALTER SYSTEM statements:

- ALTER SYSTEM FLUSH SHARED_POOL
- ALTER SYSTEM FLUSH BUFFER_CACHE
- ALTER SYSTEM ENABLE RESTRICTED SESSION
- ALTER SYSTEM DISABLE RESTRICTED SESSION
- ALTER SYSTEM SET USE_STORED_OUTLINES
- ALTER SYSTEM SUSPEND
- ALTER SYSTEM RESUME
- ALTER SYSTEM CHECKPOINT
- ALTER SYSTEM CHECK DATAFILES
- ALTER SYSTEM REGISTER
- ALTER SYSTEM KILL SESSION
- ALTER SYSTEM DISCONNECT SESSION
- ALTER SYSTEM SET initialization_parameter (for a subset of initialization parameters)

The new CON_ID column in the V$PARAMETER view contains the ID of the container to which the data pertains. Possible values include:

- **0** -- This value is used for rows containing data that pertain to the entire CDB. This value is also used for rows in non-CDBs.
- **1** -- This value is used for rows containing data that pertain to only the root
- **n** -- Where n is the applicable container ID for the rows containing data

Managing Storage in a CDB and PDBs

Manage permanent and temporary tablespaces in CDB and PDBs

Tablespaces in a multitenant environment serve the same purpose and for the most part are treated in the same fashion as tablespaces in a non-CDB. The syntax for creating and altering tablespaces is largely unchanged. There are a few considerations for tablespaces in a CDB:

- A permanent tablespace can be associated with only one container.
- When you create a tablespace in a container, the tablespace is associated with that container.
- A CDB can have only one active undo tablespace or one active undo tablespace for each instance of an Oracle RAC CDB.
- There is one default temporary tablespace for an entire CDB. The root and the PDBs can use this temporary tablespace. Optionally, each PDB can also have its own temporary tablespace.

Because a permanent tablespace can be associated with only a single container, each container must have its own default permanent tablespace. They cannot be shared between containers. Users connected to a given container who are not explicitly assigned a tablespace will use that container's default permanent tablespace. When connected to the CDB, the command to set the default permanent tablespace would be:

```
ALTER DATABASE DEFAULT TABLESPACE tbs_users_cdb;
```

While connected to a PDB, the 'ALTER DATABASE' command is still retained for backward compatibility, but the preferred command would be:

```
ALTER PLUGGABLE DATABASE DEFAULT TABLESPACE tbs_users_pdb;
```

The current settings for the default tablespaces can be determined by querying the database_properties view:

```
SELECT property_name, property_value
FROM   database_properties
WHERE  property_name like '%TABLESPACE';

PROPERTY_NAME                  PROPERTY_VALUE
------------------------------ --------------
DEFAULT_TEMP_TABLESPACE        TEMP2
DEFAULT_PERMANENT_TABLESPACE   USERS
```

A CDB will have only a single default temporary tablespace (or tablespace group). In order to create or modify this temporary tablespace, the current container must be the root. It is possible to have additional temporary tablespaces in the root, and to assign specific users to them. Likewise, each PDB can contain one default temporary tablespace and additional temporary tablespaces that can be assigned specific users. When a PDB is unplugged from a CDB, its temporary tablespaces are also unplugged.

Managing Security in a CDB and PDBs

Manage common and local users

A common user is a database user that has the same identity in the root and in every existing and future PDB. Common users can connect to and perform operations within the root, and within any PDB in which it has been granted privileges. A user connected to the root can perform certain operations, such as ALTER PLUGGABLE DATABASE, CREATE USER, CREATE ROLE, that affect other pluggable databases (PDBs). However, most privileges can only be exercised within the current container. Users must first switch to the PDB where the action is to be taken, and then exercise their privileges from there. For example, a common user cannot query tables or views in a PDB when it is not the current container.

Creating a common user account:

- You must be connected to the root and have the commonly granted CREATE USER system privilege.
- The session's current container must be CDB$ROOT.
- The name of the common user must start with C## or c## and contain only ASCII or EDCDIC characters.
- To explicitly designate a user account as a common user, in the CREATE USER statement, specify CONTAINER=ALL. When logged into the root, if the CONTAINER clause is omitted, CONTAINER=ALL is implied.

No objects should be created in the schemas of common users. They cannot be shared across PDB boundaries and can cause problems during plug-in and unplug operations. The following example creates a common user account and grants the user the SET CONTAINER and CREATE SESSION privileges (common users must have these privileges to navigate between containers):

```
CREATE USER c##ocp_admin
  IDENTIFIED BY password
  DEFAULT TABLESPACE ts_cdb_users
  QUOTA 100M ON ts_cdb_users
  TEMPORARY TABLESPACE temp_ts
  CONTAINER = ALL;
GRANT SET CONTAINER, CREATE SESSION
  TO c##ocp_admin CONTAINER = ALL;
```

Creating a local user account:

Local user accounts exist only in the PDB that they are created in. They cannot connect to or be granted privileges in other PDBs. It is possible, of course, to create a user of the same name in multiple PDBs, but the accounts share nothing except the name. To create a local user account:

- You must be connected to the PDB in which you want to create the account, and have the CREATE USER privilege.
- The name of the local user must not start with C## or c##.
- The clause CONTAINER=CURRENT can be included in the CREATE USER statement to explicitly specify the user as a local user. When connected to a PDB, if the clause is omitted, CONTAINER=CURRENT is implied.

```
CREATE USER ocp_user
  IDENTIFIED BY password
  DEFAULT TABLESPACE ts_pdb_users
  QUOTA 100M ON ts_pdb_users
  TEMPORARY TABLESPACE temp_ts
  PROFILE ocp_profile
  CONTAINER = CURRENT;
```

Manage common and local privileges

Common users and local users can grant privileges to one another. A given privilege (i.e. CREATE ANY TABLE) is neither common nor local by itself. If CREATE ANY TABLE is granted commonly, then it becomes a common privilege, and if granted locally, it becomes a local privilege.

Commonly granted privileges:

- A privilege that is granted commonly can be used in every existing and future container.
- Only common users can grant privileges commonly, and only to a common user or a common role.
- The grantor must be connected to the root and must specify CONTAINER=ALL in the GRANT statement.
- Can include system and object privileges.
- Should never be granted to PUBLIC.

Locally granted privileges:

- A privilege granted locally can be used only in the container in which it was granted, even when granted in the root.
- Both common users and local users can grant privileges locally.
- A common user and a local user can grant privileges to other common or local roles.
- The grantor must be connected to the container and must specify CONTAINER=CURRENT in the GRANT statement.
- Any user can grant a privilege locally to any other user or role (both common and local) or to the PUBLIC role.

The CONTAINER clause in a GRANT or REVOKE statement determines where a privilege is granted to or revoked from. When the CONTAINER is set to ALL, the statement applies the privilege to all existing and future containers. Using CURRENT in the clause will apply the privilege to the local container. The value will default to CURRENT if the clause is omitted except when connected to the root, when the default will be ALL. The following example grants the CREATE TABLE privilege to common user c##ocp_admin. After the grant, the user will be able to use the privilege in all existing and future containers.

```
GRANT CREATE TABLE TO c##ocp_admin CONTAINER=ALL;
```

Manage common and local roles

Common roles are created in the root and are known in all existing and future containers. All Oracle-supplied predefined roles are common roles. Local roles exist in only the PDB they were created in and can only be used there. Local roles cannot have any commonly granted privileges.

- Common users can both create and grant common roles to other common and local users.
- A common role can be granted to a common user either commonly or locally.
- If a common role is granted to a local user, the privileges from the role apply only to the local user's PDB.
- Local users cannot create common roles
- Local users can grant common roles to common and local users.

If the following requirements are met, commonly granted privileges that have been made to a common role apply in the root and all current and future PDBs to which the grantor can connect:

- Both the grantor and the grantee are common users.
- The grantor possesses the commonly granted SET CONTAINER privilege and the ADMIN OPTION for the common role.
- The GRANT statement contains the CONTAINER=ALL clause.

The name given to user-created common roles must start with C## or c## and contain only ASCII or EDCDIC characters (the C## rule does not apply to Oracle-supplied roles, such as DBA or RESOURCE). When the role is created, the CONTAINER clause must be set to ALL. Except when logged in to the root, omitting this clause from the CREATE ROLE statement creates a local role in the current PDB. If the CONTAINER clause is omitted when logged in to the root, by default the role is created as a common role. The following example creates the c##ocp_admin common role:

```
CREATE ROLE c##ocp_admin CONTAINER=ALL;
```

Enable common users to access data in specific PDBs

The CONTAINER clause of a GRANT statement can be used to grant a privilege to a specific PDB in a multitenant environment. When a privilege is granted while connected to the root, setting CONTAINER to the PDB name applies the privilege to the specified PDB only. The following example would grant the SELECT ANY TABLE privilege to common user c##hr_admin to the ocp_pdb PDB while connected to the root:

```
GRANT SELECT ANY TABLE TO c##ocp_admin CONTAINER=ocp_pdb;
```

Except while connected to the root, omitting the CONTAINER clause applies the privilege to the local container. If a GRANT statement for an object is made by a local user while connected to a given PDB, then the privilege is applied to that PDB only. Either of the following statements would grant the SELECT ANY TABLE privilege to common user c##ocp_admin to the ocp_pdb PDB while connected to that PDB:

```
GRANT SELECT ANY TABLE TO c##ocp_admin;
GRANT SELECT ANY TABLE TO c##ocp_admin CONTAINER=CURRENT;
```

Container Data Objects

A container data object is a table or view that contains information about multiple containers and possibly the CDB as a whole. In a multitenant environment, the X$ tables and the V$, GV$ and CDB_* views are examples of container data objects. Querying these objects can return information about the root and every PDB in the container database. It is possible to restrict data pertaining to one or more containers when common users perform queries of these objects. This may be necessary to avoid exposing sensitive information about specific PDBs to common users. All container data objects have a CON_ID column that indicates which container a particular row references. This column can contain the following values:

- **0** -- Whole CDB, or non-CDB
- **1** -- CDB$ROOT
- **2** -- PDB$SEED
- **Other #s** -- User-Created PDBs

In order to enable common users to access data about specific PDBs, they must be assigned the appropriate CONTAINER_DATA value. This is done by executing an ALTER USER statement from the root. The following example enables the common user c##ocp_admin to view information pertaining to the CDB$ROOT, OCP_PDB, and DEV_PDB containers in all container data objects accessible to that user, for the V$SESSION view.

```
ALTER USER c##ocp_admin
SET CONTAINER_DATA = (CDB$ROOT, OCP_PDB, DEV_PDB)
FOR V$SESSION CONTAINER=CURRENT;
```

The CONTAINER = CURRENT clause must be specified. When connected to the root, CONTAINER=ALL is the default for the ALTER USER statement, but modification of the CONTAINER_DATA attribute must be restricted to the root.

Managing Availability

Perform backups of a CDB and PDBs

There is a full range of capabilities for backing up Oracle databases in a multitenant environment through RMAN and Enterprise Manager Cloud Control. If is possible to back up and recover a complete CDB, just the root of the CDB, or to back up any or all of the PDBs. It is also possible to back up and recover individual tablespaces and data files in a single PDB. Backing up each element of a container database individually (the root and each PDB) is functionally equivalent in terms of recoverability to backing up the entire CDB.

The steps for backing up an entire CDB are equivalent to performing a full database backup of a non-CDB. When the entire CDB is backed up, RMAN backs up the root, all the PDBs, and the archived redo logs. From the resulting backup, it is possible to recover the whole CDB, the root only, or combination of PDBs contained in the CDB backup. To back up a CDB, you must start RMAN and connect to the root of the CDB as a common user with the SYSBACKUP or SYSDBA privilege and to a recovery catalog (if used). The database must be either mounted or open. You can then issue the appropriate backup options from the RMAN prompt:

Back up the entire CDB:

```
RMAN> BACKUP DATABASE;
```

Back up the database, switch the online redo logs, and include archived logs in the backup:

```
RMAN> BACKUP DATABASE PLUS ARCHIVELOG;
```

Back Up the Root

```
RMAN> BACKUP DATABASE ROOT;
```

Back Up a PDB

There are two approaches to backing up a PDB with RMAN:

- Connect to the root and then issue the BACKUP PLUGGABE DATABASE command from the RMAN prompt. This method can be used to back up one or more PDBs.

  ```
  RMAN> BACKUP PLUGGABLE DATABASE ocprep;

  RMAN> BACKUP PLUGGABLE DATABASE ocprep, testdb;
  ```

- Connect to the PDB and then issue the following command from the RMAN prompt:

  ```
  RMAN> BACKUP DATABASE;
  ```

Recover PDB from PDB datafiles loss

When recovering a container database, it is possible to recover the entire CDB, only the root, only a single PDB, or just a portion of a PDB such as a tablespace or datafile. When the whole CDB is recovered, the root and all PDBs are recovered in a single operation.

To recover the entire CDB, you use the RMAN commands RESTORE and RECOVER. RMAN will automatically restore the backups of any required archived redo logs during the recovery operation. If the backup is stored on a media manager, then any required channels must be configured so that RMAN can access the backup files. To recover an entire CDB, you must start RMAN and connect to the root of the CDB as a common user with the SYSBACKUP or SYSDBA privilege and to a recovery catalog (if used). The following commands will restore and recover the entire CDB:

```
RESTORE DATABASE;
RECOVER DATABASE;
```

You can delete any archived redo logs that were restored from disk for the recovery operation (once they are no longer needed for recovery) by using the following command:

```
RECOVER DATABASE DELETE ARCHIVELOG;
```

It is possible to recover only the root if a user error or data corruption occurs that is specific to the root. However, Oracle strongly recommends that you recover all PDBs after recovering the root. This will eliminate the possibility of introducing metadata inconsistencies among the root and the PDBs. As a general rule, it is preferable to recover the whole CDB. To recover the root, you must be connected to the root from RMAN as a common user with the SYSDBA or SYSBACKUP privilege and the CDB must be in MOUNT mode.

- If required, use the CONFIGURE command to configure the default device type and automatic channels.
- Restore and recover the root with the following commands:

  ```
  RESTORE DATABASE ROOT;
  RECOVER DATABASE ROOT;
  ```

- Examine the output from RMAN to verify that media recovery was successful. Oracle strongly recommends at this point that you recover all of the PDBs, including the seed. To do this, issue the RESTORE PLUGGABLE DATABASE and RECOVER PLUGGABLE DATABASE commands.

  ```
  RESTORE PLUGGABLE DATABASE 'PDB$SEED', ocprep, testdb;
  RECOVER PLUGGABLE DATABASE 'PDB$SEED', ocprep, testdb;
  ```

- Examine the output from RMAN to verify that media recovery was successful. If it was successful, open the CDB and all PDBs.

  ```
  ALTER DATABASE OPEN;
  ALTER PLUGGABLE DATABASE ALL OPEN;
  ```

It is possible to perform a complete recovery on a given PDB, or multiple PDBs without affecting operations of other open PDBs in the same container database. It is possible to recover a PDB in RMAN while connected to the root or while connected to the PDB. While connected to the root, you would use the RESTORE PLUGGABLE DATABASE and RECOVER PLUGGABLE DATABASE commands (as shown in the example above). With these commands, you can recover multiple pluggable databases at once. When connected to the PDB you would use the RESTORE DATABASE and RECOVER DATABASE commands. Only one PDB can be recovered at a time using this method. The following steps will recover the ocprep PDB while connected to the root from RMAN as a common user with the SYSDBA or SYSBACKUP privilege:

- Close the PDBs to be recovered.

```
ALTER PLUGGABLE DATABASE ocprep CLOSE;
```

- If the PDB has missing data files an error will occur and the PDB cannot be closed. You must connect to the PDB with missing data file(s) and take them offline so that the PDB can be closed. The following command takes the data file 8 offline:

```
ALTER PLUGGABLE DATABASE DATAFILE 8 OFFLINE;
```

- If required, use the CONFIGURE command to configure the default device type and automatic channels.
- Restore and recover the PDB with the following commands:

```
RESTORE PLUGGABLE DATABASE ocprep;
RECOVER PLUGGABLE DATABASE ocprep;
```

- If any data files were taken offline in Step 2, bring these data files back online, for example:

```
ALTER PLUGGABLE DATABASE DATAFILE 8 ONLINE;
```

- Examine the output from RMAN to verify that media recovery was successful. If it was successful, open the PDB(s).

```
ALTER PLUGGABLE DATABASE ocprep OPEN;
```

To recover a single PDB while connected to it, you connect to the PDB from RMAN as a local user with SYSDBA system privilege.

- Close the PDB.

```
ALTER PLUGGABLE DATABASE CLOSE;
```

- If the PDB has missing data files an error will occur and the PDB cannot be closed. You must connect to the PDB with missing data file(s) and take them offline so that the PDB can be closed. The following command takes the data file 8 offline:

```
ALTER DATABASE DATAFILE 8 OFFLINE;
```

- If required, use the CONFIGURE command to configure the default device type and automatic channels.
- Restore and recover the PDB with the following commands:

```
RESTORE DATABASE;
RECOVER DATABASE;
```

- If any data files were taken offline in Step 2, connect to that PDB and bring these data files back online, for example:

```
ALTER DATABASE DATAFILE 8 ONLINE;
```

- Examine the output from RMAN to verify that media recovery was successful. If it was successful, open the PDB(s).

```
ALTER PLUGGABLE DATABASE OPEN;
```

Use Data Recovery Advisor

Oracle's Data Recovery Advisor is a data corruption repair function integrated with Support Workbench, database health checks and RMAN. It can display data corruption problems, assess their extent and impact, recommend repair options, and automate the repair process. In the context of Data Recovery Advisor, a health check is a diagnostic procedure run by the Health Monitor to assess the state of the database or its components. Health checks are invoked reactively when an error occurs and can also be invoked manually. Data Recovery Advisor can diagnose failures such as the following:

- Components such as data files and control files that are not accessible by the database.
- Physical corruptions such as block checksum failures and invalid block header field values.
- Inconsistencies such as a data file that is older than other database files.
- I/O failures such as hardware errors, operating system driver failures, and exceeding operating system resource limits.

In some cases, the Data Recovery Advisor may be able to detect or handle logical corruptions. As a general rule, detecting and repairing logical corruptions will require assistance from Oracle Support Services.

Failures

A failure is a persistent data corruption detected by a health check. They are usually detected reactively when a database operation encounters corrupted data and generates an error. This will automatically invoke a health check in the database. The check will search the database for failures related to the error and record any findings in the Automatic Diagnostic Repository. Data Recovery Advisor can generate repair advice and repair failures only after failures have been detected by the database and stored in the ADR. Data Recovery Advisor can report on and repair failures such as inaccessible files, physical and logical block corruptions, and I/O failures. All failures are assigned a priority: CRITICAL, HIGH, or LOW, and a status of OPEN or CLOSED.

- **CRITICAL** priority failures require immediate attention because they make the whole database unavailable. Typically, critical failures bring down the instance and are diagnosed during the subsequent startup.

- **HIGH** priority failures make a database partially unavailable or unrecoverable, and usually have to be repaired in a reasonably short time.
- **LOW** priority indicates that failures can be ignored until more important failures are fixed.

DRA Repairs

Data Recovery Advisor allows you to view repair options. Repairs might involve the use of block media recovery, datafile media recovery, or Oracle Flashback Database. In general, Data Recovery Advisor presents both automated and manual repair options. If appropriate, you can choose an automated repair option in order to perform a repair. In an automated repair, Data Recovery Advisor performs the repair, verifies the repair success, and closes the relevant failures.

The recommended workflow for repairing data failures from RMAN is to run the following commands in sequence during an RMAN session: LIST FAILURE to display failures, ADVISE FAILURE to display repair options, and REPAIR FAILURE to fix the failures.

LIST FAILURE

The LIST FAILURE command displays failures against which you can run the ADVISE FAILURE and REPAIR FAILURE commands.

```
RMAN> LIST FAILURE;
List of Database Failures
=========================
Failure ID Priority Status  Time Detected Summary
---------- -------- ------- ------------- ----------------------
274        HIGH     OPEN    21-FEB-14     One or more non-system
                                          datafiles are missing
329        HIGH     OPEN    21-FEB-14     Datafile 1:
                                          '/u01/oradata/prod/
                                           system01.dbf'
                                          contains one or more
                                          corrupt blocks
```

ADVISE FAILURE

Use the ADVISE FAILURE command to display repair options for the specified failures. This command prints a summary of the failures identified by the Data Recovery Advisor and implicitly closes all open failures that are already fixed. The ADVISE FAILURE command indicates the repair strategy that Data Recovery Advisor considers optimal for a given set of failures. Data Recovery Advisor verifies repair feasibility before proposing a repair strategy. For example, it will check that all backups and archived redo log files needed for media recovery are available. It can generate both manual and automated repair options.

The ADVISE command maps a set of failures to the set of repair steps that Data Recovery Advisor considers to be optimal. When possible, Data Recovery Advisor consolidates multiple repair steps into a single repair. For example, if the database has corrupted datafile, missing control file, and lost current redo log group, then Data Recovery Advisor would recommend a single, consolidated repair plan to restore the database and perform point-in-time recovery.

```
RMAN> ADVISE FAILURE;
List of Database Failures
=========================
Failure ID Priority Status   Time Detected Summary
---------- -------- -------- ------------- ----------------------
274        HIGH     OPEN     21-FEB-14     One or more non-system
                                           datafiles are missing
329        HIGH     OPEN     21-FEB-14     Datafile 1:
                                           '/u01/oradata/prod/
                                             system01.dbf'
                                           contains one or more
                                           corrupt blocks

analyzing automatic repair options; this may take some time
using channel ORA_DISK_1
analyzing automatic repair options complete

Mandatory Manual Actions
========================
no manual actions available

Optional Manual Actions
=======================
```

```
1. If file /u01/oradata/prod/data01.dbf was unintentionally renamed
or moved, restore it

Automated Repair Options
========================
Option Repair Description
--- ---------
Restore and recover datafile 31; Perform block
    media recovery of block 43481 in file 1

Strategy: The repair includes complete media recovery with no data
loss
Repair script:
/u01/oracle/log/diag/rdbms/prod/prod/hm/reco_740113269.hm
```

CHANGE FAILURE

The CHANGE FAILURE command allows you to change the failure priority from HIGH to LOW or the reverse, or to close it. You cannot change to or from CRITICAL priority.

```
RMAN> CHANGE FAILURE 3 PRIORITY LOW;
```

REPAIR FAILURE

The REPAIR FAILURE command is used to repair database failures identified by the Data Recovery Advisor. The target database instance must be started. It must be a single-instance database and cannot be a physical standby database. It is important that at most one RMAN session is running the REPAIR FAILURE command. The only exception is REPAIR FAILURE ... PREVIEW, which is permitted in concurrent RMAN sessions. To perform an automated repair, the Data Recovery Advisor may require specific backups and archived redo logs. If the files are not available, then the recovery will not be possible. Data Recovery Advisor consolidates repairs whenever possible so that a single repair can fix multiple failures. If one has not yet been issued in the current RMAN session, REPAIR FAILURE performs an implicit ADVISE FAILURE. RMAN always verifies that failures are still relevant and automatically closes failures that have already been repaired. After executing a repair, RMAN reevaluates all open failures on the chance that some of them may also have been fixed.

Duplicate PDBs using RMAN

The DUPLICATE command of RMAN can be used to duplicate PDBs. It is possible to duplicate a single PDB, a set of PDBs, or a set of tablespaces within a PDB. This action must be performed while logged in to the root of the CDB as a user with the SYSDBA or SYSBACKUP privilege. In order to duplicate PDBs, it is required to create the auxiliary instance as a CDB by starting the instance with the declaration enable_pluggable_database=TRUE in the initialization parameter file.

When one or more PDBs is duplicated, RMAN will also duplicate the root (CDB$ROOT) and the seed database (PDB$SEED). The result after the duplication operation is a separate database that is a fully functional CDB. The options that can be used when duplicating PDBs or tablespaces within PDBs are:

- **PLUGGABLE DATABASE pdb_name** -- Duplicates the specified PDBs in the CDB. Use a comma-delimited list to duplicate multiple PDBs.
- **SKIP PLUGGABLE DATABASE pdb_name** -- Duplicates all the PDBs in the CDB, except the PDBs specified by pdb_name. Use a comma-delimited list to specify multiple PDBs that must be excluded.
- **TABLESPACE pdb_name:tablespace_name** -- Duplicates specified tablespaces within a PDB. The tablespace name must be prefixed with the name of the PDB that contains the tablespace. If you omit the name of the PDB, root is taken as the default.
- **SKIP TABLESPACE pdb_name:tablespace_name** -- Duplicates all tablespaces in the CDB except the specified tablespaces in the specified PDB.

The steps to duplicate a PDB are:

1. Start RMAN and connect to the necessary database instances.
2. If the source database instance is not mounted or open, then mount or open it. To perform duplication of an open database, it must have archiving enabled.
3. Configure RMAN channels (if necessary).
4. Run the DUPLICATE command with either the PLUGGABLE DATABASE or SKIP PLUGGABLE DATABASE option. Some examples include:
    - Duplicate the PDB pdb1 to the CDB cdb1::

      ```
      DUPLICATE DATABASE TO cdb1
        PLUGGABLE DATABASE pdb1;
      ```

    - Duplicate the PDBs pdb1, pdb3, and pdb4 to the database cdb1:

      ```
      DUPLICATE DATABASE TO cdb1
        PLUGGABLE DATABASE pdb1,pdb3,pdb4;
      ```

    - Duplicate all the databases in the CDB, except the PDB pdb3:

      ```
      DUPLICATE DATABASE TO cdb1
        SKIP PLUGGABLE DATABASE pdb3;
      ```

The steps to duplicate tablespaces within a PDB are:

1. Start RMAN and connect to the necessary database instances.
2. If the source database instance is not mounted or open, then mount or open it. To perform duplication of an open database, it must have archiving enabled.
3. Configure RMAN channels (if necessary).

4. Run the DUPLICATE command with the TABLESPACE option. Some examples of duplicating tablespaces contained in PDBs are:
    - Duplicate the users tablespace that is part of PDB pdb1:

```
DUPLICATE DATABASE TO cdb1
  TABLESPACE pdb1:users;
```

    - Duplicate the PDB pdb1 and the users tablespace in PDB pdb2:

```
DUPLICATE DATABASE TO cdb1
  PLUGGABLE DATABASE pdb1
  TABLESPACE pdb2:users;
```

Managing Performance

Monitor operations and performance in a CDB and PDBs

There are a significant number of tools and techniques for identifying performance issues. One of the easiest in recent releases of Oracle has been to use Enterprise Manager. In 12c, there is Enterprise Manager Cloud Control, Oracle's enterprise information technology management product. EM Cloud Control is designed to manage entire IT environments, including databases, server, middleware products and more. The kid brother of EM Cloud Control is EM Express.

EM Express is a web-based tool for managing Oracle Database 12c that is built into the database server. It is a lightweight tool designed to incur minimal overhead on the database server and provides the ability to perform basic administrative tasks as well as the ability to diagnose performance issues and tune the database. There are no background tasks or information-collecting processes associated with EM Express. The tool makes use of data that is already collected by the Oracle database. The Performance Hub of EM Express is going to be the 'go to' spot for many administrators in 12c for diagnosing performance issues. The image below shows the main page of the EM Express Performance Hub.

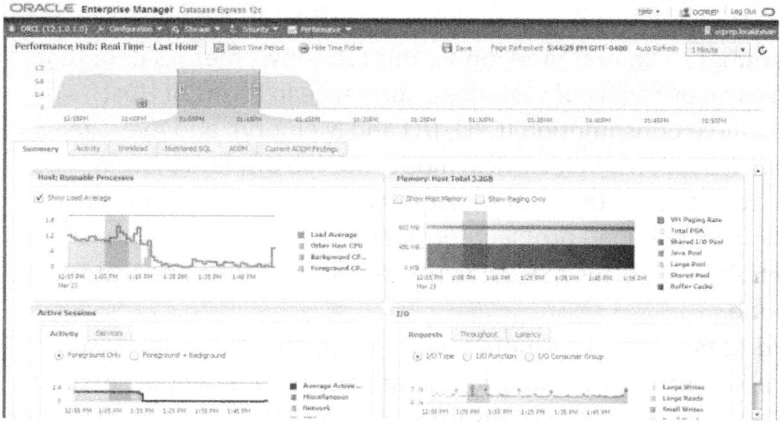

The Performance Hub provides a consolidated view of all performance data for a given time range. The performance data shown includes ASH Analytics, SQL Monitor, ADDM, as well as metrics that describe workload characteristics and database resource usage.

The Performance Hub can be used to view both historical and real-time data. A time range can be selected using a time picker at the top of the page, and the detail tabs will display the available performance data for the selected time range. The time picker displays average active sessions over time. When there are peaks in the time picker, the selected time range can be moved to the period of interest to gain more information.

When functioning in real-time mode, performance data is retrieved from in-memory views. The time picker shows data for the past hour and the user can select any time range from within this period. The default selection is the past 5 minutes. When functioning in historical mode, data is retrieved from the Automatic Workload Repository (AWR). The user can select any time period, provided there is sufficient data in AWR. The Performance Hub can also be saved as a Composite Active Report.

The Performance Hub organizes performance data by dividing it into different tabs that address a specific aspect of database performance. The tabs available in the Performance Hub are:

- **Summary** -- In real-time mode, this tab shows metrics data that gives an overview of system performance in terms of Host Resource Consumption (CPU, I/O and Memory), and Average Active Sessions. In historical mode, the tab displays system performance in terms of resource consumption, average active sessions, and load profile information.
- **Activity** -- Displays ASH Analytics in both real-time and historical mode.
- **Workload** -- Displays metric information about the workload profile, such as call rates, logon rate and the number of sessions. In addition, the tab also displays the Top SQL for the selected time range. In real-time mode, the tab displays Top SQL only by DB

time. In historical mode, the user can also display Top SQL by other metrics, such as CPU time or Executions.

- **RAC** -- Displays RAC-specific metrics such as the number of global cache blocks received, and the average block latency when the database is in a RAC configuration.
- **Monitored SQL** -- Displays Monitored Executions of SQL, PL/SQL and Database Operations in both real-time and historical mode.
- **ADDM** -- Displays ADDM and Automatic Real Time ADDM reports in both real-time and historical mode.
- **Current ADDM Findings** -- Displays a real-time analysis of system performance for the past 5 minutes. The tab is available only in real-time mode and the contents of this tab are populated only if the time selector includes the current time.

Manage allocation of resources between PDBs and within a PDB

The Oracle Database Resource Manager (DRM) is designed to optimize resource allocation among concurrent database sessions. It attempts to prevent problems that can happen if the operating system makes resource decisions when presented with high overhead without having awareness of the database needs. DRM helps to overcome these problems by giving the database more control over how hardware resources are allocated. DRM enables you to classify sessions into groups based on session attributes, and then allocate resources to those groups in a way that optimizes hardware utilization for your application environment. The information that performs the functions of classifying sessions and assigning resources is called a resource plan. Oracle 12c comes with several predefined resource plans that provide resource management directives that should provide immediate benefits for the majority of database installations:

- **DEFAULT_MAINTENANCE_PLAN** -- Default plan for maintenance windows.
- **DEFAULT_PLAN** -- Basic default plan that prioritizes SYS_GROUP operations and allocates minimal resources for automated maintenance and diagnostics operations.
- **DSS_PLAN** -- Example plan for a data warehouse that prioritizes critical DSS queries over non-critical DSS queries and ETL operations.
- **ETL_CRITICAL_PLAN** -- Example plan for a data warehouse that prioritizes ETL operations over DSS queries.
- **INTERNAL_QUIESCE** -- For quiescing the database. This plan cannot be activated directly. To activate, use the QUIESCE command.
- **MIXED_WORKLOAD_PLAN** -- Example plan for a mixed workload that prioritizes interactive operations over batch operations.

There are three elements of DRM:

- **Resource consumer group**: A group of sessions that are grouped together based on resource requirements.
- **Resource plan**: A container for directives that specify how resources are allocated to resource consumer groups.
- **Resource plan directive**: Associates a resource consumer group with a particular plan and specifies how resources are to be allocated to that resource consumer group.

Resource Plan Directives

A resource plan directive for a consumer group can specify limits for CPU and I/O resource consumption for sessions in that group. This is done by specifying the action to be taken if a call within a session exceeds one of the specified limits. These actions, called switches, occur only for sessions that are running and consuming resources, not waiting for user input or for CPU cycles. The possible actions are the following:

- The session is switched to a consumer group with lower resource allocations.
- The session is killed (terminated).
- The session's current SQL statement is aborted.

The resource plan directive attribute that determines which of the above three actions will be taken is SWITCH_GROUP. This attribute specifies the consumer group to which a session is switched if the specified criteria are met. If the value of this parameter is a consumer group, the session will be switched to that group. If the group name is 'CANCEL_SQL', the current call for that session is canceled. Finally, if the group name is 'KILL_SESSION', then the session is killed.

Per session I/O or CPU Limits

The resource plan directive attributes that can be used in specifying the criteria to use in making switch determinations follow. If not set, all default to UNLIMITED.

- **SWITCH_TIME**: Specifies the time (in CPU seconds) that a call can execute before an action is taken.
- **SWITCH_IO_MEGABYTES**: Specifies the number of megabytes of I/O that a session can transfer (read and write) before being switched.
- **SWITCH_IO_REQS**: Specifies the number of I/O requests that a session can execute before an action is taken.

There are two resource plan attributes that can be used to modify the behavior of resource plan switching:

- **SWITCH_ESTIMATE**: If TRUE, the database estimates the execution time of each call. If the estimated execution time exceeds SWITCH_TIME, the session is moved to the SWITCH_GROUP before beginning the call. The default is FALSE.

- **SWITCH_FOR_CALL**: If TRUE, a session that was automatically switched to another consumer group is returned to its original consumer group when the top level call completes. The default is NULL.

Resource Manager and CDBs

Competing workloads are complex enough in an Oracle database that is not using the multitenant architecture. Resource management in a CDB becomes much more complex as resources are now being shared among multiple PDBs competing for system and CDB resources. Resource Manager works on two basic levels in a CDB environment:

- **CDB level** - It manages the workloads for multiple PDBs that are competing for resources. It is possible to specify how resources should be allocated among various PDBs, and limits can be set for specific PDBs.
- **PDB level** - Workloads within each PDB can be managed.

Resources are allocated in a two-step process:

- Each PDB is allocated a portion of the total system resources in the CDB.
- Within each specific PDB, the resources obtained in the first step are allocated among the connected sessions.

The Resource Manager allows administrators to perform the following:

- Specify that different PDBs should receive varying shares of the system resources based on the relative importance of each PDB.
- Limit the CPU usage of a particular PDB
- Limit the number of parallel execution servers that a particular PDB can use
- Limit the resource usage of different sessions connected to a single PDB

- Monitor the resource usage of PDBs

Perform Database Replay

Before making significant hardware or software upgrades to a production Oracle database, typically extensive testing is performed to verify the changes will not adversely affect the system. However, making such testing close enough to reality to provide a valid test is very difficult. Often problems are encountered after the upgrade that were not located during the testing period. There are various third-party tools on the market to provide load testing for Oracle, simulating the workload from multiple users. However, the workloads generated are not as complex and interactive as that generated by a real production system. The Database Replay feature enables system administrators to perform real-world testing by capturing the production database workload and replaying it on another database. In addition, it provides analysis and reporting of potential problems and recommend ways to resolve these problems.

Oracle Database Replay captures all external database calls made to the system during the workload capture period. The capture includes all relevant information about the client request, such as SQL text, bind values, and transaction information. Background activities of the database and scheduler jobs are not captured. In addition, the following types of client requests are not captured in a workload:

- Direct path load of data from external files using utilities such as SQL*Loader
- Shared server requests (Oracle MTS)
- Oracle Streams
- Advanced replication streams
- Non-PL/SQL based Advanced Queuing (AQ)
- Flashback queries
- Oracle Call Interface (OCI) based object navigations
- Non SQL-based object access
- Distributed transactions

It is a best practice to restart the database before capturing the production workload. This ensures that ongoing and dependent transactions are allowed to be completed or rolled back before the capture begins. If the database is not restarted before the capture, transactions that are in progress or have yet to be committed will be only partially captured in the workload.

By default, all activities from all user sessions are recorded during workload capture. Workload filters can be used to include or exclude specific user sessions during the workload capture. You can use either inclusion filters or exclusion filters in a workload capture, but not both simultaneously. Inclusion filters specify user sessions that will be captured in the workload. Exclusion filters enable you to specify user sessions that will not be captured in the workload. To add filters to a workload capture, you use the DBMS_WORKLOAD_CAPTURE.ADD_FILTER procedure. To remove an existing filter, you use the DBMS_WORKLOAD_CAPTURE.DELETE_FILTER procedure.

Before starting the workload capture, you must decide on the directory where the captured workload will be stored. Before starting the capture, verify that the directory is empty and has enough space for the workload. If the directory runs out of disk space during a workload capture, the capture will stop. You should have a well-defined starting point for the workload so that the database being used to replay the workload can be restored to the same point before starting the captured workload. It is best not to have any active user sessions when starting a workload capture. Active sessions may have ongoing transactions which will not be replayed completely. Consider restarting the database in RESTRICTED mode prior to starting the workload capture. When the workload capture begins, the database will automatically switch to UNRESTRICTED mode and normal operations can continue while the workload is being captured. You begin a workload capture using the procedure DBMS_WORKLOAD_CAPTURE.START_CAPTURE. To stop a workload capture in progress, you use the FINISH_CAPTURE procedure of the DBMS_WORKLOAD_CAPTURE package.

You can export AWR data from the production machine in order to enable detailed analysis of the workload on both systems. This data is required if you plan to run the AWR Compare Period report on a pair of workload captures or replays. To export AWR data, you use the DBMS_WORKLOAD_CAPTURE.EXPORT_AWR procedure.

The following views allow you to monitor a workload capture. You can also use Oracle Enterprise Manager to monitor a workload capture:

- **DBA_WORKLOAD_CAPTURES** -- Lists all the workload captures that have been created in the current database.
- **DBA_WORKLOAD_FILTERS** -- Lists all workload filters used for workload captures defined in the current database.

Replay

After the workload has been captured, it's necessary to preprocess the capture files prior to using them in a replay. Preprocessing converts the captured data into replay files and creates the required metadata needed to replay the workload. After preprocessing the captured workload, it can be replayed multiple times on any replay system running the same version of Oracle. As a general rule, it's recommended to move the capture files to another system for preprocessing. While the capture itself has a minimal overhead, workload preprocessing can be time consuming and resource intensive. It is better that this step be performed on the test system where the workload will be replayed rather than on the production database. Capture files are processed using the PROCESS_CAPTURE procedure of the DBMS_WORKLOAD_REPLAY package.

After you have preprocessed a captured workload, it can be replayed on the test system. In the workload replay, Oracle will perform the actions recorded during the workload capture. It will re-create all captured external client requests with the same timing, concurrency, and transaction dependencies that occurred on the production system.

Database Replay uses a program called the replay client to re-create the external client requests. You may need to use multiple replay clients depending on the scope of the captured workload. The replay client has an imbedded calibration tool to help determine the number of replay clients required for a given workload. The entire workload from the production database is replayed. This includes DML and SQL queries, so the data in the replay system must be as logically similar to the data in the capture system as possible. Ensuring the systems are as identical as possible will minimize data divergence and enable a more reliable analysis of the replay. Replaying a database workload requires the following steps:

The captured workload must have been preprocessed and copied to the replay system. An Oracle directory object for the directory to which the preprocessed workload has been copied must exist in the replay system.

A captured workload may contain references to external systems, such as database links or external tables. These should be reconfigured to avoid impacting production systems during replay. External references that need to be resolved before replaying a workload include: Database links, external tables, directory objects, URLs, and e-mail addresses. If these external connections are not changed before starting the replay, you could end up changing data in production systems, sending emails to users, and other undesirable actions.

Connection strings used to connect to the production system are captured in the workload. You must remap these connection strings to the replay system for the replay to succeed. The clients can then connect to the replay system using the remapped connections. For Oracle Real Application Cluster databases, you can map all connection strings to a load balancing connection string.

There are several options that determine the behavior of the database replay.

- **synchronization** -- determines whether the COMMIT order will be preserved during replay. By default, synchronization is enabled. All transactions will be executed only after all dependent transactions have been committed. If you disable this option, the replay will likely have significant data divergence. This may be not be a problem if the workload consists primarily of independent transactions. Not preserving the commit order can also lead to a faster replay, if 'stress testing' of the replay system is desirable.
- **connect_time_scale** -- enables you to scale the elapsed time between the time when the sessions connected to the database during the workload capture began and when each session connects during the replay. This option allows you to manipulate the session connect time during replay with a given percentage value. By default, the value is 100, which will attempt to connect all sessions as captured. Setting this parameter to 0 will attempt to connect all sessions immediately.
- **think_time_scale** -- allows you to scale user think time during replay. User think time is the elapsed time while the replayed user waits between issuing calls within a single session. A value of 100 means that time between calls will be the same as they were during the capture. A value of zero will eliminate all wait time between calls.
- **think_time_auto_correct** -- If user calls are being executed slower during replay than during capture, you can make the database replay attempt to catch up by setting this parameter to TRUE. When set to true, it will make the replay client shorten the think time between calls, so that the overall elapsed time of the replay will more closely match the captured elapsed time.

The replay client is a multithreaded program where each thread submits a workload from a captured session. It is an executable file named wrc located in the $ORACLE_HOME/bin directory. The replay user that wrc logs in as needs the DBA role and cannot be SYS. The wrc executable uses the following syntax:

```
wrc [user/pword[@server]] MODE=[value] [keyword=[value]]
```

The mode parameter specifies the action to be taken when the wrc executable is run. Possible values include replay (the default), calibrate, and list_hosts. The parameter keyword specifies the options to use for the execution and is dependent on the mode selected. To display the possible keywords and their corresponding values, run the wrc executable without any arguments. The modes that you can select when running the wrc executable and their corresponding keywords are:

- **replay (the default)** -- runs a captured workload. In replay mode, the wrc executable accepts the following keywords:
    - **userid and password** -- specify the user ID and password of a replay user for the replay client. If unspecified, the user ID defaults to the SYSTEM user.
    - **server** -- specifies the connection string that is used to connect to the replay system. If unspecified, the value defaults to an empty string.
    - **replaydir** -- specifies the directory that contains the preprocessed workload capture you want to replay. If unspecified, it defaults to the current directory.
    - **debug** -- specifies whether debug data will be created.
    - **workdir** -- specifies the directory where the client logs will be written. This parameter is only used in conjunction with the debug parameter.
    - **connection_override** -- specifies whether to override the connection mappings stored in the DBA_WORKLOAD_CONNECTION_MAP view.
- **calibrate** -- causes wrc to return an estimate of the number of replay clients and hosts that are required to replay a particular workload. In calibration mode, wrc accepts the following keywords:
    - **replaydir** -- specifies the directory that contains the preprocessed workload capture. It defaults to the current directory.
    - **process_per_cpu** -- specifies the maximum number of client processes that can run per CPU. The default value is 4.
    - **threads_per_process** -- specifies the maximum number of threads that can run within a client process. The default value is 50.

- **list_hosts** -- Displays the hosts that participated in a workload capture and workload replay. In list_hosts mode, the wrc executable accepts only one keyword:
  - replaydir -- specifies the directory that contains the preprocessed workload capture you want to replay. If unspecified, it defaults to the current directory

Once the workload replay has completed, in-depth reporting is available so that you can perform detailed analysis of both the workload capture and the replay operation. The summary report provides basic information such as errors encountered during replay and data divergence in rows returned by DML or SQL queries. A comparison of several statistics between the source and replay servers is also provided. You can use Automatic Workload Repository reports for advanced analysis of the workload processing between the two servers.

Moving Data, Performing Security Operations and Interacting with Other Oracle Products

Use Data Pump

The Oracle Data Pump utility is designed to provide high-speed movement of data and metadata from one database to another. It replaces the export/import functionality that existed in earlier releases of Oracle. Data Pump is made up of three distinct parts:

- **expdp and impdp** – These are command-line clients that use the procedures provided in the DBMS_DATAPUMP package to execute export and import commands. They accept parameters entered at the command line that enable the exporting and importing of data and metadata for a complete database or for subsets of a database.
- **DBMS_DATAPUMP** – Also known as the Data Pump API, this package provides a high-speed mechanism to move all or part of the data and metadata for a site from one database to another. DBMS_DATAPUMP can be used independently of the impdp and expdp clients.
- **DBMS_METADATA** – Also known as the Metadata API, this package provides a centralized facility for the extraction, manipulation, and re-creation of dictionary metadata. DBMS_METADATA can be used independently of the impdp and expdp clients.

Data Pump jobs use a master table, a master process, and worker processes to perform the work and keep track of progress:

- **Master Table** – A master table is used to track the progress within a job while the data and metadata are being transferred. It is implemented as a user table within the database. A user performing an impdp or expdp must have the CREATE TABLE system privilege for the master table to be created plus sufficient tablespace quota. The master table will have the same name as the job that created it. A Data Pump job cannot have the same name as an existing table or view in that schema. The information in the master table is used to restart a job.

- **Master process** – A master process is created for every Data Pump Export job and Data Pump Import job. It controls the entire job, including communicating with the clients, creating and controlling a pool of worker processes, and performing logging operations.
- **Worker Process** – The master process allocates work to be executed to worker processes that perform the data and metadata processing within an operation. Data Pump can employ multiple worker processes, running in parallel, to increase job performance.

Monitor a Data Pump job

It's possible to use the Data Pump Export and Import utilities to attach to a running job. When attached in logging mode, status about the job is automatically displayed during execution in real-time. When attached using interactive-command mode, it's possible to request the job status.

Optionally, a log file can be written during the execution of a job. It summarizes the progress of the job, lists any errors, and records the completion status. You can also determine job status or to get other information about Data Pump jobs, through the Data Pump views:

- **DBA_DATAPUMP_JOBS** – Identifies all active Data Pump jobs in the database, regardless of their state, on an instance (or on all instances for RAC). It also shows all Data Pump master tables not currently associated with an active job.
- **DBA_DATAPUMP_SESSIONS** – Identifies the user sessions that are attached to a Data Pump job. The information in this view is useful for determining why a stopped Data Pump operation has not gone away.
- **V$SESSION_LONGOPS** – Data Pump operations that transfer table data (export and import) maintain an entry indicating the job progress. The entry contains the estimated transfer size and is periodically updated to reflect the actual amount of data transferred.

The V$SESSION_LONGOPS columns that are relevant to a Data Pump job are as follows:

- **USERNAME** - job owner
- **OPNAME** - job name
- **TARGET_DESC** - job operation
- **SOFAR** - megabytes transferred thus far during the job
- **TOTALWORK** - estimated number of megabytes in the job
- **UNITS** - megabytes (MB)
- **MESSAGE** - a formatted status message of the form: 'job_name: operation_name : nnn out of mmm MB done'

The Data Pump Export utility is invoked using the expdp command. The actions performed by the export operation are defined by the parameters you specify. They can be supplied either on the command line or in a parameter file. Data Pump Export can be controlled using a command line, a parameter file, or an interactive-command mode.

- **Command-Line** – Enables you to specify most of the export parameters from the command line.
- **Parameter File** – Allows you to specify command-line parameters in a parameter file. The PARFILE parameter cannot be used in a parameter file, because parameter files cannot be nested.
- **Interactive-Command** – Displays an export prompt from which you can enter various commands. Some commands are specific to interactive-command mode.

Data Pump jobs manage the following types of files:

- **Dump files** – Contain the data and metadata being moved.
- **Log files** – Record the messages associated with an operation.
- **SQL files** – Record the output of a SQLFILE operation.
- **Data Files** – Files specified by the DATA_FILES parameter during a transportable import.

There are different expdp modes for unloading different portions of the database. The mode is specified using the appropriate parameter. The available modes are:

- **Full** – In a full database export, the entire database is unloaded. This mode requires the user performing the export to have the DATAPUMP_EXP_FULL_DATABASE role. Specified using the FULL parameter.
- **Schema** – This is the default export mode. If you have the DATAPUMP_EXP_FULL_DATABASE role, then you can provide a list of schemas to export. Otherwise you can export only your own schema. Specified using the SCHEMAS parameter.
- **Table** – In table mode, only a specified set of tables, partitions, and their dependent objects are unloaded. You must have the DATAPUMP_EXP_FULL_DATABASE role to export tables that are not in your own schema. Specified using the TABLES parameter.
- **Tablespace** – In tablespace mode, only the tables contained in a specified set of tablespaces are unloaded. If a table is unloaded, then its dependent objects are also unloaded. Privileged users get all tables. Unprivileged users get only the tables in their own schemas. Specified using the TABLESPACES parameter.
- **Transportable Tablespace** – In transportable tablespace mode, only the metadata for the tables (and their dependent objects) within a specified set of tablespaces is exported. The tablespace data files are copied in a separate operation. Specified using the TRANSPORT_TABLESPACES parameter.

expdp Parameters

The following parameters are applicable to expdp:

- **ATTACH** – Attaches the client session to an existing export job and automatically places you in the interactive-command interface.
- **CONTENT** – Enables you to filter what Export unloads: data only, metadata only, or both.
- **DIRECTORY** – Specifies the default location to which Export can write the dump file set and the log file.

- **DUMPFILE** – Specifies the names, and optionally, the directory objects of dump files for an export job.
- **ESTIMATE** – Specifies the method that Export will use to estimate how much disk space each table in the export job will consume (in bytes).
- **ESTIMATE_ONLY** – Instructs Export to estimate the space that a job would consume, without actually performing the export operation.
- **EXCLUDE** – Enables you to filter the metadata that is exported by specifying objects and object types to be excluded from the export operation.
- **FILESIZE** – Specifies the maximum size of each dump file.
- **FULL** – Specifies that you want to perform a full database mode export.
- **INCLUDE** – Enables you to filter the metadata that is exported by specifying objects and object types for the current export mode.
- **JOB_NAME** – Used to identify the export job in subsequent actions.
- **LOGFILE** – Specifies the name, and optionally, a directory, for the log file of the export job.
- **PARFILE** – Specifies the name of an export parameter file.
- **QUERY** – Allows you to specify a query clause that is used to filter the data that gets exported.
- **SCHEMAS** – Specifies that you want to perform a schema-mode export.
- **TABLES** – Specifies that you want to perform a table-mode export.
- **TABLESPACES** – Specifies a list of tablespace names to be exported in tablespace mode.
- **TRANSPORT_TABLESPACES** -- Specifies that you want to perform an export in transportable-tablespace mode. This parameter is used to specify a list of tablespace names for which object metadata will be exported from the source database into the target database.

impdp Parameters

Many of the above parameters are also applicable to impdp. In addition, several of the more common impdp parameters are:

- **REUSE_DATAFILES** – Specifies whether the import job should reuse existing data files for tablespace creation.
- **SQLFILE** – Specifies a file into which all of the SQL DDL that Import would have executed, based on other parameters, is written.
- **STATUS** – Specifies the frequency at which the job status display is updated.
- **TABLE_EXISTS_ACTION** – Tells import what to do if the table it is trying to create already exists.
- **REMAP_DATAFILE** – Changes the name of the source data file to the target data file name in all SQL statements where the source data file is referenced.
- **REMAP_SCHEMA** – Loads all objects from the source schema into a target schema.
- **REMAP_TABLE** – Allows you to rename tables during an import operation.
- **REMAP_TABLESPACE** – Remaps all objects selected for import with persistent data in the source tablespace to be created in the target tablespace.

The following commands are applicable when using Interactive mode:

- **ADD_FILE** – Add additional dump files.
- **CONTINUE_CLIENT** – Exit interactive mode and enter logging mode.
- **EXIT_CLIENT** – Stop the import or export client session, but leave the job running.
- **KILL_JOB** – Detach all currently attached client sessions and terminate the current job.
- **PARALLEL** – Increase or decrease the number of active worker processes for the current job.
- **START_JOB** – Restart a stopped job to which you are attached.
- **STATUS** – Display detailed status for the current job and/or set status interval.

- **STOP_JOB** – Stop the current job for later restart.

Network-based Data Pump operations

When the NETWORK_LINK parameter is used with impdp as part of an import operation, data is moved directly using SQL. A SELECT clause retrieves the data from the remote database using the network link supplied with the parameter. A corresponding INSERT clause inserts the data into the target database. No dump files are involved in the operation. When the NETWORK_LINK parameter is used with expdp as part of an export operation, data from the remote database is written to dump files on the target database. A 'Current User' database link is not supported for use with Data Pump. Only the following types of database links are supported:

- Public (both public and shared)
- Fixed user
- Connected user

There are some restrictions for operations performed using the NETWORK Link parameter:

- When using full transportable export, tables with LONG or LONG RAW columns that reside in administrative tablespaces (such as SYSTEM or SYSAUX) are not supported.
- When transporting a database over the network using full transportable export, auditing cannot be enabled for tables stored in an administrative tablespace (such as SYSTEM and SYSAUX) if the audit trail information itself is stored in a user-defined tablespace.
- The source and target databases can differ by no more than two versions. For example, if one database is Oracle Database 12c, then the other database must be 12c, 11g, or 10g.

Oracle 12c Enhancements

When performing a full database export, Data Pump has a new full transportable export option. A full transportable export is performed when the TRANSPORTABLE=ALWAYS parameter is specified along with the FULL parameter. This functionality exports all objects and data required to create a complete copy of the database. Two data movement methods are performed by Data Pump depending on whether the tablespaces are transportable or not:

- **Non-transportable tablespaces** -- Tablespaces like SYSTEM and SYSAUX that cannot be transported have both their metadata and data unloaded into the dump file set, using direct path unload and external tables.
- **Transportable tablespaces** -- For transportable tablespaces, only metadata unloaded into the dump file set. The contents of the tablespaces are moved when you the data files are copied to the target database.

There are several restrictions for performing a full transportable export, including:

- The DATAPUMP_EXP_FULL_DATABASE privilege is required to perform this operation.
- The default tablespace of the user performing the export must not be set to one of the tablespaces being transported.
- If the database being exported contains either encrypted tablespaces or tables with encrypted columns, the ENCRYPTION_PASSWORD parameter must be supplied.
- If there are encrypted tablespaces in the source database, the source and target databases must be on platforms with the same endianness.
- If the source platform and the target platform are of different endianness, then you must convert the data being transported so that it is in the format of the target platform.
- A full transportable export is not restartable.
- All objects with storage that are selected for export must have all of their storage segments either entirely within administrative,

non-transportable tablespaces (SYSTEM / SYSAUX) or entirely within user-defined, transportable tablespaces. Storage for a single object cannot straddle the two kinds of tablespaces.

The new functionality can be used to move a non-CDB into a pluggable database (PDB) or to move a PDB into another PDB. Full transportable operations can reduce both the export time and import times required for a full export. When this option is used, table data does not need to be unloaded and reloaded and index structures in user tablespaces do not need to be re-created. The full transportable feature is ideal for moving a database to a new computer system or upgrading to a new release of Oracle.

There are two enhancements to the way Data Pump works with compression.

- **Compression on import** -- A new option has been added to impdp and to the DBMS_DATAPUMP package that allows the compression options for a table to be changed during the import operation. The TRANSFORM parameter of impdp has a new TABLE_COMPRESSION_CLAUSE. If NONE is specified, the table gets the default compression for the tablespace. When the value is a valid table compression clause (for example, NOCOMPRESS), tables are created with the specified compression. Specifying this transform changes the type of compression for all tables in the job.
- **Compression on export** -- A new option has been added expdp and the DBMS_DATAPUMP package to control the degree of compression used when creating an Oracle Data Pump dump file. The COMPRESSION parameter can be used to compress the entire operation, the data only, the metadata only, or perform no compression. By default, only the metadata is compressed. The new parameter allows the DBA more control over the resources used during an export operation.

Other enhancements to Data Pump include:

- **Export View As a Table** -- A new expdp command-line option will cause Data Pump to export a view as a table. Rather than exporting the view definition, Data Pump will export a table definition and unload data from the view as if it were a table. When the dump file is imported, impdp will create a table using the table definition and insert the data
- **LOGTIME** -- The new LOGTIME command-line parameter will cause messages displayed during export and import operations be timestamped. The option is available in impdp, expdp, and the DBMS_DATAPUMP.SET_PARAMETER procedure. The valid values are:
  - **NONE** -- No timestamps on status or log file messages (the default)
  - **STATUS** -- timestamps on status messages only
  - **LOGTIME** -- timestamps on log file messages only
  - **ALL** -- timestamps on both status and log file messages
- **Audit Commands** -- Oracle Data Pump commands can now be audited.
- **No Logging Option** -- A new DISABLE_ARCHIVE_LOGGING option has been added to the TRANSFORM parameter of impdp and the DBMS_DATAPUMP package. When utilized, it will disable redo logging when loading data into tables and when creating indexes. When the option is used, the disk space required for redo logs during an Oracle Data Pump import will be smaller. After performing the import operation, the DBA should perform an RMAN backup. Other operations still generate redo, including CREATE and ALTER statements (except CREATE INDEX) and operations against the master table used by Oracle Data Pump.
- **Security** -- The ENCRYPTION_PWD_PROMPT parameter has been added to the expdp and impdp command line. The parameter is used to indicate whether the Oracle Data Pump client should prompt for passwords or whether it should retrieve the value from the command line.
- **SecureFiles LOB as Default** – A new option for impdp and the DBMS_DATAPUMP package forces Oracle Data Pump to create all LOBs as SecureFiles LOBs. By default, Data Pump re-creates tables exactly as they existed in the exported database, so if a LOB column was a BasicFile LOB in the exported database, Data Pump

attempts to re-create it as a BasicFile LOB in the imported database.

Use SQL*Loader

SQL*Loader is useful for loading data from non-Oracle databases. It has a very flexible data parsing engine that can handle a wide range of flat file formats when loading data. Essentially any database has the ability to export data to a flat file format. SQL*Load can then make use of these files to import the data into tables in an Oracle database. SQL*Loader can perform the following functions:

- Load data across a network if your data files are on a different system than the database.
- Load data from multiple data files during the same load session.
- Load data into multiple tables during the same load session.
- Specify the character set of the data.
- Selectively load data based on the record values.
- Manipulate data before loading it, using SQL functions.
- Generate unique sequential key values in specified columns.
- Use the operating system's file system to access the data files.
- Load data from disk, tape, or named pipe.
- Generate sophisticated error reports.
- Load arbitrarily complex object-relational data.
- Use secondary data files for loading LOBs and collections.
- Use conventional, direct path, or external table loads.

SQL*Loader can be used with or without a control file. Using a control file provides more control over the load operation. Simple load operations can be performed without specifying a control file. This is referred to as SQL*Loader express mode. SQL*Loader sessions make use of the following files:

- **Control** – Defines the format of the data file and controls the behavior of SQL*Loader.
- **Data** – One or more data files will contain the information to be loaded.
- **Log** – Contains a log of the actions performed by SQL*Loader and errors encountered.
- **Bad** – Contains all records that could not be loaded due to errors.
- **Discard** – Contains all records that the control file identified to be bypassed.

The sqlldr executable is used to invoke SQL*Loader. It is optionally followed by parameters that establish session characteristics. Parameters can also be specified using the following methods instead of the command line:

- Parameters can be added to a parameter file. To use a parameter file, the name of the file can be supplied in the command line using the PARFILE parameter.
- Some parameters can be specified within the SQL*Loader control file using the OPTIONS clause.

If the same parameter is specified on the command line and in a parameter file or OPTIONS clause, the value in the command line is used.

The SQL*Loader control file is a text file that tells SQL*Loader where to find the data file, the format to use in parsing the data, what table(s) to insert the data in to, and more. A control file has three loosely-defined sections:

- The first section contains session-wide information such as global options, the input data file location, and the data to be loaded.
- The second section consists of one or more INTO TABLE blocks. The blocks hold information about the destination table.
- The third section is optional and, if present, contains input data.

SQL*Loader has two methods of inserting data into Oracle tables, Conventional Path and Direct Load options. In conventional path, SQL*Loader effectively creates INSERT statements for the records in the file to be loaded and passes them to the Oracle SQL Parser to be handled. When using Direct Path, SQL*Loader bypasses SQL and the parser and loads data directly into the target table(s). Direct Path load is much faster, but Conventional Path is more flexible. Some restrictions of the Direct Path load are:

- It cannot run concurrently with other transactions against the target table.
- Triggers on the table do not fire.
- Data is written above the high-water mark of the table even if there is space below.
- Clustered tables are not supported.
- Foreign Key constraints are disabled during the load.

Express Mode

The new SQL*Loader express mode makes it possible to load data from a flat file by specifying only a table name. For the functionality to succeed the file must contain only delimited data and the table columns must be all character, number, or datetime types. When running in express mode, no control file is used. SQL*Loader uses the table column definitions to determine the input field order and data types in the file. For other settings, it makes use of default values unless overridden with command-line parameters. The following example performs a basic load into the EMPLOYEES table:

```
sqlldr username TABLE=employees
```

By default, SQL*Loader express mode assumes the following values unless specified otherwise:

- **Data file** -- When none is specified, SQL*Loader looks for a file named [table_name].dat in the current directory.
- **Load method** -- By default external tables is used. For some errors, SQL*Loader express mode will automatically switched to direct path load.
- **Fields** -- The fields use the names, column types, and order from the destination table. Records are delimited by a comma, separated by a newline, have no enclosure and use left-right trimming.
- **DOP** -- The DEGREE_OF_PARALLELISM parameter is set to AUTO.
- **Date Format** -- The NLS settings are used.
- **Character Set** -- The NLS settings are used.
- **Append mode --** New data is to be appended to the table if it already has data in it.
- **File Names** -- When a data file is not specified, the data, log, and bad files take the following default names. (The %p is replaced with the process ID of the Oracle Database slave process.):
    - **Data File** -- table-name.dat
    - **SQL*Loader Log File** -- table-name.log
    - **Oracle Database Log Files** -- table-name_%p.log_xt
    - **Bad File** -- table-name_%p.bad

Audit operations

The new unified audit trail in 12c consolidates audit information from multiple sources and makes this information available in a standard format in the UNIFIED_AUDIT_TRAIL data dictionary view. The unified audit trail is maintained in a read-only table in the AUDSYS schema in the SYSAUX tablespace. The data is available to SYS and to users who have been granted the AUDIT_ADMIN or AUDIT_VIEWER roles. The AUDIT_ADMIN role can view the data and create audit policies. The AUDIT_VIEWER role can query the views but not create or alter policies. In unified auditing, the audit trail combines the audit records from the following sources:

- Unified audit policies and AUDIT settings
- Fine-grained audit records from DBMS_FGA
- Oracle Database Real Application Security
- Oracle Recovery Manager
- Oracle Database Vault
- Oracle Label Security
- Oracle Data Mining
- Oracle Data Pump
- Oracle SQL*Loader Direct Load

Once configured, unified auditing is always enabled and does not depend on the initialization parameters used in previous releases. If the database is opened in READ-ONLY mode, audit records are written to new operating system files in the $ORACLE_BASE/audit/$ORACLE_SID directory. The V$OPTION view can be queried to determine whether a database has been migrated to use unified auditing:

```
SELECT value
FROM   v$option
WHERE  parameter = 'Unified Auditing';

PARAMETER         VALUE
----------------  ----------
Unified Auditing  TRUE
```

This output shows that unified auditing is enabled. If it were disabled, the query would return FALSE. For newly created 12c databases, mixed mode auditing is enabled by default through the predefined policy ORA_SECURECONFIG. Mixed-mode auditing enables both traditional (pre-12c auditing) and unified auditing. The traditional auditing capabilities are controlled by the AUDIT_TRAIL initialization parameter. When set to a value other than 'none' in 12c, the traditional audit trail will be populated with audit records and the unified audit trail will also be populated. Audit settings can be applied to individual PDBs or to the CDB as a whole, depending on the type of policy. In a Multitenant environment, each PDB, including the root, has own unified audit trail.

When a database from an older release is upgraded to 12c, it is necessary to manually migrate to unified auditing if you want to use this capability. Once unified auditing is enabled, traditional auditing is disabled. To start using unified auditing, at least one unified audit policy must be enabled. To stop using it, disable all unified audit policies. The predefined policy ORA_SECURECONFIG is initially enabled on new 12c databases. The settings for this policy are:

```
CREATE AUDIT POLICY ORA_SECURECONFIG
PRIVILEGES ALTER ANY TABLE, CREATE ANY TABLE, DROP ANY TABLE,
CREATE ANY PROCEDURE, DROP ANY PROCEDURE, ALTER ANY PROCEDURE,
GRANT ANY PRIVILEGE, GRANT ANY OBJECT PRIVILEGE, GRANT ANY ROLE,
AUDIT SYSTEM, CREATE EXTERNAL JOB, CREATE ANY JOB,
CREATE ANY LIBRARY,
EXEMPT ACCESS POLICY,
CREATE USER, DROP USER,
ALTER DATABASE, ALTER SYSTEM,
CREATE PUBLIC SYNONYM, DROP PUBLIC SYNONYM,
CREATE SQL TRANSLATION PROFILE, CREATE ANY SQL TRANSLATION PROFILE,
DROP ANY SQL TRANSLATION PROFILE, ALTER ANY SQL TRANSLATION PROFILE,
CREATE ANY SQL TRANSLATION PROFILE, DROP ANY SQL TRANSLATION PROFILE,
ALTER ANY SQL TRANSLATION PROFILE, TRANSLATE ANY SQL,
EXEMPT REDACTION POLICY,
PURGE DBA_RECYCLEBIN, LOGMINING,
ADMINISTER KEY MANAGEMENT
ACTIONS ALTER USER, CREATE ROLE, ALTER ROLE, DROP ROLE, SET ROLE,
CREATE PROFILE, ALTER PROFILE, DROP PROFILE,
CREATE DATABASE LINK, ALTER DATABASE LINK, DROP DATABASE LINK,
LOGON, LOGOFF, CREATE DIRECTORY, DROP DIRECTORY;
```

Disabling Unified Auditing

When disabling unified auditing, you should first disable any unified audit policies that are currently enabled. This will prevent the database from going into mixed mode auditing once unified auditing is disabled.

- Log into the database instance as a user with the AUDIT_ADMIN role and query the POLICY_NAME and ENABLED_OPT columns of the AUDIT_UNIFIED_ENABLED_POLICIES data dictionary view.

Execute the NOAUDIT POLICY statement to disable any policies that are enabled.

- Connect as user SYS with the SYSOPER privilege.
- Shut down the database.

```
SHUTDOWN IMMEDIATE
```

- From the command prompt, run the following commands:

```
cd $ORACLE_HOME/rdbms/lib
make -f ins_rdbms.mk uniaud_off ioracle
```

- From SQL*Plus, restart the database.

```
STARTUP
```

By default, audit records are written to system global area (SGA) queues and then periodically written to the AUDSYS schema audit table in the SYSAUX tablespace. Queuing the records rather than immediately writing them to disk significantly improves the performance of the audit trail processes. However, if there is an instance crash or a SHUTDOWN ABORT, the queued writes mean there is a chance that some audit records may be lost. If this is not acceptable, the audit trail can be set to immediately write audit records to the AUDSYS schema audit table. Be aware that on an active database that this setting may affect performance. In a multitenant database, this option can be set for individual PDBs. To set the write mode for unified audit trail records:

- Log in to SQL*Plus as a user who has been granted the AUDIT_ADMIN role.
- Set the AUDIT_TRAIL_MODE property of the DBMS_AUDIT_MGMT package, as follows:
  To use immediate-write mode, run the following procedure:

```
BEGIN
 DBMS_AUDIT_MGMT.SET_AUDIT_TRAIL_PROPERTY(
  DBMS_AUDIT_MGMT.AUDIT_TRAIL_UNIFIED,
  DBMS_AUDIT_MGMT.AUDIT_TRAIL_WRITE_MODE,
  DBMS_AUDIT_MGMT.AUDIT_TRAIL_IMMEDIATE_WRITE);
END;
```

To use queued-write mode, run the following procedure:

```
BEGIN
 DBMS_AUDIT_MGMT.SET_AUDIT_TRAIL_PROPERTY(
  DBMS_AUDIT_MGMT.AUDIT_TRAIL_UNIFIED,
  DBMS_AUDIT_MGMT.AUDIT_TRAIL_WRITE_MODE,
  DBMS_AUDIT_MGMT.AUDIT_TRAIL_QUEUED_WRITE);
END;
```

Any time that the database is not writable, including when the instance is started but the database is closed or when the database is open in read-only mode, audit records are written to external files in the $ORACLE_BASE/audit/$ORACLE_SID directory. The contents of these files can be loaded into the database by running the DBMS_AUDIT_MGMT.LOAD_UNIFIED_AUDIT_FILES procedure. The process to do this is:

- Log into the database instance as a user who has been granted the AUDIT_ADMIN role.
- Ensure that the database is open and writable.
- Run the DBMS_AUDIT_MGMT.LOAD_UNIFIED_AUDIT_FILES procedure.

```
EXEC DBMS_AUDIT_MGMT.LOAD_UNIFIED_AUDIT_FILES;
```

- The audit records are loaded into the AUDSYS schema audit table immediately, and then deleted from the $ORACLE_BASE/audit/$ORACLE_SID directory.

A unified audit policy is a named group of audit settings that track a particular aspect of user behavior in the database. The CREATE AUDIT POLICY statement is used to create a unified audit policy. More than one audit policy can be in effect concurrently in a database. They can contain both system-wide and object-specific audit options. The AUDIT and NOAUDIT SQL statements enable and disable an audit policy respectively. The AUDIT statement can also be used to include or exclude specific users for the given policy. The AUDIT and NOAUDIT statements also enable you to audit application context values. The following types of activities can be audited:

- User accounts (including administrative users who log in with the SYSDBA administrative privilege), roles, and privileges.
- Object actions, such as dropping a table or a running a procedure
- Application context values
- Activities from Oracle Database Real Application Security, Oracle Recovery Manager, Oracle Data Mining, Oracle Data Pump, Oracle SQL*Loader direct path events, Oracle Database Vault, and Oracle Label Security

It is possible to have multiple policies enabled concurrently, but ideally the number of enabled policies should be limited. The unified audit policy syntax is flexible enough to allow one policy to cover a number of audit settings. The best practice is to group related options into a single policy rather than creating multiple policies. Having a small number of policies reduces the logon overhead associated with loading audit policy details into the session's UGA memory. The session's UGA memory consumption is also reduced and the internal audit check functionality is more efficient.

When a unified audit policy is generated with the CREATE AUDIT POLICY statement, Oracle Database stores it in a first class object that is owned by the SYS schema, rather than the schema of the user who created the policy. The basic syntax for the CREATE AUDIT POLICY statement is:

```
CREATE AUDIT POLICY policy_name
{ {privilege_audit_clause [action_audit_clause ] [role_audit_clause
]}
| { action_audit_clause [role_audit_clause ] }
| { role_audit_clause }
}
[WHEN audit_condition EVALUATE PER {STATEMENT|SESSION|INSTANCE}]
[CONTAINER = {CURRENT | ALL}];
```

The following statement creates a policy that would generate an audit trail any time a statement requiring the ALTER ANY TABLE or DROP ANY TABLE system privileges granted via the ocp_admin role was executed.

```
CREATE AUDIT POLICY change_table_pol
PRIVILEGES ALTER ANY TABLE, DROP ANY TABLE
ROLES ocp_admin;
```

Once the policy has been created, it must be enabled using the AUDIT statement with the POLICY clause. The policy can be applied to one or more users, or to all users with specified exclusions. It is also possible to designate whether an audit record is written when the audited action succeeds, fails, or regardless of whether the action succeeds.

Newly-created policies will not take effect until after the audited user's next connection to the database instance. If the audited users are logged in when a policy is enabled, the policy cannot collect audit data until the users log out and back in to the database. The AUDIT statement supports the following optional clauses:

- **BY** -- Used to apply the unified audit policy to one or more users.

  ```
  AUDIT POLICY change_table_pol BY ocpuser;
  ```

- **EXCEPT** -- Used to exclude users from the unified audit policy.

  ```
  AUDIT POLICY change_table_pol EXCEPT jtkirk, jlpicard;
  ```

- **WHENEVER SUCCESSFUL** -- Records only successful executions of the audited activity.

  ```
  AUDIT change_table_pol WHENEVER SUCCESSFUL;
  ```

- **WHENEVER NOT SUCCESSFUL** -- Records only failed executions of the audited activity.

  ```
  AUDIT change_table_pol WHENEVER NOT SUCCESSFUL;
  ```

Note the following:

- **WHENEVER** -- If the WHENEVER clause is omitted, the both failed and successful user activities are written to the audit trail.
- **BY/EXCEPT** -- A unified audit policy can be enabled with either the BY clause or the EXCEPT clause, but not both simultaneously.

- **AUDIT...BY** -- If multiple AUDIT statements are executed on the same unified audit policy with different BY users, all of the specified users are audited.
- **AUDIT...EXCEPT** -- If multiple AUDIT statements are executed on the same unified audit policy with different EXCEPT users, only the last exception user list is used.
- **COMMON policies** -- Common unified audit policies can only be enabled from the root and only for common users.
- **LOCAL policies** -- Local audit policies can only be enabled from the PDB to which it applies.

Use Other Products with CDB and PDBs - Database Vault, Data Guard, LogMiner

Database Vault

In order to use Oracle Database Vault in a multitenant environment, you must register it in the root first. Once Oracle Database Vault has been registered in the root, it can be registered in the PDBs. An attempt to register it in a PDB first will result in the error "ORA-47503: Database Vault is not enabled on CDB$ROOT.

The first step in registering Database Vault is to log into the root of the database instance as a user who has privileges to create users and grant the CREATE SESSION and SET CONTAINER privileges. Ideally you should create two accounts to be used for Database Vault accounts and grant both the CREATE SESSION and SET CONTAINER privileges. The first account will be for the Database Vault Owner user. The second is optional, but recommended. If created, it will be the Database Vault Account Manager account. Both accounts should have at minimum the CREATE SESSION privilege. If a Database Vault Account Manager account is not created, the owner account will have the Database Vault Account Manager privileges. Oracle recommends creating both accounts for better separation of duties. Since both accounts will be common users, their names should be prefixed with c## or C##. For example:

```
GRANT CREATE SESSION, SET CONTAINER TO c##dbv_owner_root
   IDENTIFIED BY password CONTAINER = ALL;
GRANT CREATE SESSION, SET CONTAINER TO c##dbv_acctmgr_root
   IDENTIFIED BY password CONTAINER = ALL;
```

Once the account(s) have been created, you must connect to the root as SYS with the SYSDBA administrative privilege and execute the DVSYS.CONFIGURE_DV procedure:

```
BEGIN
 DVSYS.CONFIGURE_DV (
   dvowner_uname          => 'c##dbv_owner_root',
   dvacctmgr_uname        => 'c##dbv_acctmgr_root');
 END;
```

Once the procedure completes, execute the utlrp.sql script to recompile invalidated objects in the root. After the objects are recompiled, connect to the root using the Database Vault Owner account that was just configured. Execute the DBMS_MACADM.ENABLE_DV procedure to enable Database Vault. Then connect to the root with SYSDBA privileges and restart the database:

```
BEGIN
  DBMS_MACADM.ENABLE_DV;
END;
```

Once Database Vault has been configured in the root, it is possible to register the common users in specific PDBs or in every PDB in the CDB. To register the users in specific PDBs, you must connect to each PDB individually and grant the CREATE SESSION and SET CONTAINER privileges to the users.

```
GRANT CREATE SESSION, SET CONTAINER TO c##dbv_owner_root;
GRANT CREATE SESSION, SET CONTAINER TO c##dbv_acctmgr_root;
```

To grant them access to all PDBs in the CDB, you would instead use the following syntax:

```
GRANT CREATE SESSION, SET CONTAINER TO c##dbv_owner_root
    IDENTIFIED BY password CONTAINER = ALL;
GRANT CREATE SESSION, SET CONTAINER TO c##dbv_acctmgr_root
    IDENTIFIED BY password CONTAINER = ALL;
```

Regardless which of the two methods are used, you must go into each PDB that is to be registered with database vault and perform the following steps (which are the same as the root example above except for the container they are run in):

1. Execute the DVSYS.CONFIGURE_DV procedure
2. Run the utlrp.sql script
3. Execute the DBMS_MACADM.ENABLE_DV
4. Restart the PDB

Data Guard

Oracle's Data Guard has full support for the Multitenant database architecture. It is possible to create a physical standby of a container database in the same fashion as a regular primary database. There are some differences that must be considered when a administering the physical standby for a CDB, including the following:

- The database role is defined at the CDB level, not by individual container.
- If a switchover or failover operation is performed, it affected the entire CDB.
- DDL related to role changes and recovery must be executed in the root container.
- To administer a multitenant environment, you must have the CDB_DBA role.
- Oracle recommends that the standby database have its own keystore.

- The redo must be shipped to the root container of the standby database.

LogMiner

It is possible to use LogMiner in a multitenant container database. However, there are several differences to be aware of when using LogMiner in a CDB. When used in a container database, several views used by LogMiner contain an additional column named CON_ID. The CON_ID column identifies the container ID that is associated with the session for which information is being displayed. When any of the views is queried from a pluggable database (PDB), only rows from that PDB will be displayed. The views affected by this change include:

- V$LOGMNR_DICTIONARY_LOAD
- V$LOGMNR_LATCH
- V$LOGMNR_PROCESS
- V$LOGMNR_SESSION
- V$LOGMNR_STATS

There are also a number of new views available that are equivalent to legacy DBA_ views. The DBA views show information for sessions defined in the container from which they are queried. The new CDB views contain a CON_ID column and show information for all containers when queried from the root. The views affected by this and the new CDB view include:

- DBA_LOGMNR_LOG -> CDB_LOGMNR_LOG
- DBA_LOGMNR_PURGED_LOG -> CDB_LOGMNR_PURGED_LOG
- DBA_LOGMNR_SESSION -> CDB_LOGMNR_SESSION

The V$LOGMNR_CONTENTS view and its associated functions are restricted to the root container in a CDB. The view has had several new columns added:

- **CON_ID** -- This column contains the ID associated with the container from which the query is executed.
- **SRC_CON_NAME** -- When mining is performed with a current LogMiner dictionary, this column contains the PDB name.
- **SRC_CON_ID** -- This column contains the container ID of the PDB that generated the redo record.
- **SRC_CON_DBID** -- When mining is performed with a current LogMiner dictionary, this column contains the PDB identifier.
- **SRC_CON_GUID** - When mining is performed with a current LogMiner dictionary, this column contains the GUID associated with the PDB.

The syntax for enabling and disabling database-wide supplemental logging is the same as in a non-CDB database. However, in a CDB, minimal supplemental logging affects the entire CDB. All other levels of supplemental logging can be controlled at the PDB level. You must be connected to the PDB to issue the commands. Supplemental logging operations that are started with CREATE TABLE or ALTER TABLE statements can be executed from either the root or a PDB. They will affect only the table to which they are applied.

It is not possible to take a dictionary snapshot for an entire CDB in a single flat file. A snapshot can be taken of a single PDB in a flat file when connected to it. It is only possible to mine the redo logs for the changes associated with the PDB whose data dictionary is contained within the flat file.

ABOUT THE AUTHOR

Matthew Morris is an Oracle Database Administrator and Developer currently employed as a Database Engineer with Computer Sciences Corporation. Matthew has worked with the Oracle database since 1996 when he worked in the RDBMS support team for Oracle Support Services. Employed with Oracle for over eleven years in support and development positions, Matthew was an early adopter of the Oracle Certified Professional program. He was one of the first one hundred Oracle Certified Database Administrators (version 7.3) and in the first hundred to become an Oracle Certified Forms Developer. In the years since, he has upgraded his Database Administrator certification for releases 8i, 9i, 10g, 11g and 12c, become an Oracle Advanced PL/SQL Developer Certified Professional and added the Expert certifications for Application Express, SQL, and SQL Tuning.

Made in the USA
Monee, IL
04 November 2026

67378118R00138